SuperParenting

Child Rearing for the New Millennium

SuperParenting
Child Rearing for the New Millennium

William Maxwell · Mary E Maxwell
Ruth Leilani Smith · Jim Pearce

Changing-Times.net
Phoenix, Arizona, USA

First edition, November 2005

Changing-Times.net
PO Box 39651
Phoenix, Arizona 85069 USA
www.changing-times.net

Printed in the United States of America

ISBN 0-9741930-2-X Pbk.

Contents

Preface and Acknowledgements		8
Foreword		11
Introduction		13

Part I   **Some General Principles**

Chapter 1	Obey the Laws of the Universe	18
Chapter 2	Make the Home Orderly	21
Chapter 3	Shower the Child with Love	25
Chapter 4	Allow the Child Independence	30
Chapter 5	Teach Your Child Justice	33
Chapter 6	Teach Your Child to Think	36

Part II   **Some Specific Suggestions to Consider Prior to Conception**

Chapter 7	Choose a Mate with Healthy Genes	42
Chapter 8	Be Chaste Before Marriage	45
Chapter 9	Conceive In Wedlock	49
Chapter 10	Love the Other Parent	52
Chapter 11	Strengthen the Mother's Body	54

Part III   **Some Specific Suggestions after Conception**

Chapter 12	The Mother Takes No Drugs	58
Chapter 13	The Father to Keep the Mother's Mind Peaceful	61
Chapter 14	The Mother to Obtain a Complete Medical Examination	65
Chapter 15	Inspire the Mother	68
Chapter 16	Pray for the Embryo	71

Part IV   **Some Specific Suggestions During Birth**

Chapter 17	Use a Birthing Stool, Squat or Water Birth	75
Chapter 18	No Drugs During Birthing	78
Chapter 19	Monitor the Birthing Room Temperature	81
Chapter 20	Lights Out, Please	83
Chapter 21	Wait for the Umbilical Cord to Collapse Before Cutting	85
Chapter 22	Suck the Throat Clear	89
Chapter 23	Don't Spank	91

Part V   **Some Specific Suggestions for Immediately after Birth and the First Year**

Chapter 24	Bathe Gently	94
Chapter 25	Let the Mother Cuddle the Infant Immediately	96
Chapter 26	Feed Colostrum to the Infant and Breast-feed	98
Chapter 27	Both Mother and Father to Sleep with the Baby	101
Chapter 28	Mother and Father to Avoid Sex in Baby's Presence	103

Chapter 29 Train the Infant's Senses   104
Chapter 30 Help the Infant Train Its Sense of Balance   106
Chapter 31 Begin Ear Training   108
Chapter 32 Wean Gently   110
Chapter 33 Expose the Child to a Wide Circle of Affections   112
Chapter 34 Keep the Infant Clean   115

Part VI   Some Specific Suggestions from Year One

Chapter 35 Name Things for Infants   118
Chapter 36 Let the Child Name Things   120
Chapter 37 Assist the Child to Master Language   122
Chapter 38 Parents to Avoid Behavior the Produces the Autocratic Personality 126

Part VII   Some Specific Suggestions from Age Two

Chapter 39 Insist Upon Neatness and Order   130
Chapter 40 Encourage the Child to Share   132
Chapter 41 Teach the Child Human Relationships   134
Chapter 42 Teach Manners   136
Chapter 43 Treat the Child as Learner   138

Part VIII Some Specific Suggestions from Age Three

Chapter 44 Treat the Child as a Mathematician (Not Arithmetician)   142
Chapter 45 Expose the Child to Scientific Puzzles   144
Chapter 46 Expose the Child Gradually to a Multicultural Nursery School   146
Chapter 47 Expose the Child to a Wide Variety Of Games   149
Chapter 48 Have a Story Time   153
Chapter 49 Have a Music Time   155
Chapter 50 Have a Happy Home   157

References   158
Illustrations   169
About the Authors   170

I showed the book to the mother of a young girl. She read the book and liked it very much. She remarked that every mother should get a copy of [this] book.

Edward de Bono, M.D., D.Psy., Ph.D., Piccadilly, London, England

This book distills insights and inspiration from the wisdom of many religions and philosophies around the world, and enriches it with scientific research. All readers will enjoy and benefit from this book.

Professor Ron Crocombe, Professor Emeritus, University of the South Pacific, Suva, Fiji (Living in the Cook Islands)

If you can only have one book on parenting, this is the one to own.

Larry Sobel, M.D., MPH, FAAFP, practicing family physician, Phoenix, Arizona

Dr. Maxwell's latest book: *SuperParenting* is the ideal handbook for the new or hopeful parent, containing best-practice advice from remote cultures to common sense, with guidance from the practical to the spiritual – a must read for every new parent (or engaged couple).

Dominic Pistillo, President and Founder
University of Advancing Technology, Tempe, Arizona

This book inspires us to take a fresh look at the roles of parents and their stewardship of children. It moves from depiction of an orderly home as a protective emotional context for children to prenatal and postnatal practical, heart-warming suggestions for nurturing children emotionally and intellectually. Gems of advice are embedded even in captions of its illustrations. It is a ground-breaking book, a pleasure to read.

Bud B. Khleif, Former Professor of Sociology, Harvard University and Professor of Sociology Emeritus, University of New Hampshire

Being part of the generation that is having children late in life lends itself to thinking one knows it all and has seen it all when it comes to the do's and don't's of pregnancy and child rearing. However, after reading Bill Maxwell's and his co-author's findings in *SuperParenting,* it opened my husband's and my eyes to new options and approaches we never heard of and look forward to integrating those ideas into our child's life.

Ellen M. Zavian, Professor of Sport Law, George Washington University

The original stimulus for this book was that the Jaycees of Fiji needed a speaker for their annual general convention in Lautoka, Fiji. Somehow, I chose to speak about my students' and my recent research at the University of the South Pacific on children's intelligence. The essence of that research was that almost any positive activity (reading to the child, playing games with the child, taking the child on excursions, etc.) over a few months' time will have measurable intelligence-improving consequences. That research contradicted the then-prevailing view in Fiji (and almost everywhere else in the world) that one's IQ is fixed.

My theme at that Jaycees convention, that intelligence scores are relatively easily enhanced, (and also easily depressed by negative treatments), sparked a most enthusiastic response in that very "modern thinking" group of young men and women. Several asked whether we could recommend a book that would instruct them, laypersons that they were, on how to improve or enhance the general intelligence of their children.

I promised to seek out such a book in the university library back in Suva, Fiji. To our surprise there was, at that time, 1978, no such book available. So, we hurriedly wrote the earlier version of this book in a matter of a few months. Fiji's largest newspaper, *The Fiji Times*, type-set and printed the volume and Desai Bookshops, Fiji's largest, featured the book in its front display window on Victoria Parade, the main street of Suva.

That original book was an attempt to state in simple language some of the timeless "secrets" of expert child rearing. My wife, the late Mary Elizabeth Maxwell, R.N., and I tried to summarize "the wisdom of the ages" with respect to conceiving and rearing children and to distill some of the most important and useful ideas contained in the scholarly literature on child-development. Both of us were impressed by the insights of Maria Montessori, one of the early pioneers of the scientific study of early-childhood training and education, and whose status in history is yet to be acknowledged by the academic mainstream.

We also drew upon Mary Maxwell's training and experiences in public health in various cultures, including at St. Elizabeth's Hospital in Washington, D.C., at the Frances Payne Bolton School of Nursing at Case

Western Reserve University, Cleveland, Ohio; in immigrant neighborhoods in Cleveland; among the Bannock and Shoshone Indian cultures in Idaho; in the fascinating Micronesian cultures, particularly in the Caroline Islands; and in Korea. My research supporting a doctoral project, "The Planning and Establishment of a Model Child-Development Center in North Carolina," (Harvard University,1967), provided much of the structure for this book and the two earlier versions.

The designing of that child-development center was the major activity of the Learning Institute of North Carolina, the nation's first exclusive "think tank" for education, in the year 1966-67. That child development center in Greensboro was initially funded by the U.S. Office of Economic Opportunity as a model preschool for North Carolina, which had no publicly funded kindergartens at that time. In designing that center, I had the advice of Professor Glenn Nimnich, then at Northern Colorado University; the constant support, coaching, and encouragement of Dr. Mary Louise Keister, then Chair of Home Economics at the University of North Carolina, Greensboro; the professional staff at the Learning Institute, and of my doctoral committee at the Harvard Graduate School of Education, chaired by Dr. Bud B. Khleif.

We must acknowledge much assistance for all three versions of this book. The late Hugo V. Neuhaus, Jr. of Houston, Texas, financed my parenting workshops in the Houston area in the 1980s and a large portion of the costs of rewriting and printing of an earlier version of this book. In 2004, The University of Advancing Technology in Tempe, Arizona, encouraged me to discharge my own current perception of my "true calling," which is to stimulate greater interest in the parenting role as the fundamental building block of civilization. A colleague at that University, JoAnn McCay, assisted with the research and proof-read the manuscript. Larry Sanford and Brian Lewis, of Poway and Oceanside, California, made many valuable suggestions for the final product. My second co-author, Ms. Ruth Leilani Smith, scanned and edited the second edition and made numerous substantive suggestions that improved this edition. The third co-author, Jim Pearce of the University of Advancing Technology, considerably enhanced the book with attractive illustrations that elevate the quality of the book to almost the status of visual art. Jim Pearce inspired the publisher and me to see the book as telling a story visually, as well as verbally. The final product reflects the publisher's strong interest in this subject and the publisher's professional and artistic sensitivities.

My teachers, those who directly influenced the tone and substance of this book, include Professor Robert Rosenthal, former Chair, Department of Psychology, Harvard University, particularly his classic, *Pygmalion in the Classroom*; Professor Edward de Bono, Rhodes Scholar, M.D., Ph.D.; Carl Dolce, Professor of Educational Administration at Harvard and Dean, School of Education, North Carolina State University. The Former Commission of Education, Harold Howe III, who brought me to North Carolina for Governor Terry Sanford's educational "think tank," the first in the U.S., and the late James Maraj, the Vice Chancellor, University of the South Pacific. Many thanks also to Professor Emeritus Ron Crocombe of the University of the South Pacific and Gordon Dryden of New Zealand, author of *The Learning Revolution*, for their insightful evaluations of the manuscript and helpful recommendations for it's improvement. As if to revive the myth of "The Muses", Sue Emmel of upstate New York brought several supporting references to our attention after we thought the book had been completed. Ms. Emmel and all of our manuscript readers made the book a manifestation of the power of consultative thinking.

Each photograph is gratefully acknowledged and its source identified. Several people read the manuscripts of the previous versions of this book at various stages of their development and made helpful comments to us, particularly Irma Gray of San Antonio, Texas. The authors assume responsibility for any error of fact or of interpretation.

William Maxwell
Ed.D. Professor of Thinking
University of Advancing Technology
maxwell@superparenting.net
Tempe, Arizona
September, 2005

As I was reading through the manuscript of this book in order to prepare the foreword, I showed the book to the mother of a young girl. She read the book and liked it very much. She remarked that every mother should get a copy of the book. Although I am a father myself, I trust that mothers's judgement more than my own as my children are now grown up and my sense of need is less acute.

To make a success of a book like this there is a need for a special blend of knowledge, cleverness, wisdom and practicality.

There is a need for knowledge to access both traditional methods and the findings of the latest research. What is put forward in this book is an important blend of both aspects. The book also crosses different cultures to learn something from each culture.

There is a need for cleverness of analysis and perception. From the knowledge and traditions there is a need to distill specific points and to assemble those into useful advice.

There is a great need for wisdom in order to put things into perspective. There is a need to see the whole picture and this includes the parents as well as the children. Wisdom is like the colour balance on a movie camera. You need to get the colour balance right in order to get a true picture of reality. Wisdom also means not going overboard with the fashions of the moment. These need to be put into perspective amongst other ideas and approaches.

Finally there is a need for practicality. Without practicality the book is no more use than an academic text which is only of interest to academics. This book is very practical. The choice of chapters and chapter headings reflects this practicality.

Putting all these things together means that the book is readable and understandable. It also means that the reader will take from the book much sound advice and help. Too often it is assumed that since having children is biologically determined, that bringing up children is a natural instinct that all mothers have and so know what to do. Sadly this is a mistaken view. In the smaller communities of bygone days there were always the older women and grandmothers to pass on the wisdom of ages. Today mothers are more on their own and have to figure things out for themselves. So a book of this sort is a great help and almost essential.

I have known Bill Maxwell for many years. I first met him when he was teaching my thinking methods in Fiji. He started the International Conference on Thinking which is still going twenty five years later. He combines a good mind with a lot of energy and enthusiasm. He is also interested in "making things happen" which is a rather rare quality in academics. I feel he is the ideal person to have undertaken the production of this book. I feel he has done a magnificent job and I am sure the reader will come to the same conclusion. Even if you only dip into the book you will find much of value.

Edward de Bono, M.D., D.Psy., Ph.D.
Piccadilly, London, England

Who are the inventors of civilization?

Among those who have debated this question are darwinists and social biologists who maintain that civilization is a product of natural evolution. The prominent historian Arnold Toynbee argued that the source of civilization is fundamentally religious in nature. One leading sociologist, Emile Durkheim, gave more weight to economic factors to explain the advancement of cultures and societies. Even some geographers offer evidence that climate factors determine when humans are predisposed to study and meditate, two preconditions for the rise of civilization.

Recently, the debate has taken a surprising turn. There is a growing body of evidence that one of the primary inventors of the pillars of civilization is children. This fundamental re-thinking about the genesis of civilization was foreshadowed by William James, one of the fathers of American psychology, and Noam Chomsky, whose linguistic theories revolutionized the way scholars think about the growth of language ("All babies 'speak' the same language up to 18 months" for example).

Some of the evidence for the belief that children are the primary inventors of civilization comes from the study of the role that children's games play in the development of the human intellect. A child's will to play is universal and universally recognized. Given the right circumstances, children begin inventing games shortly after birth ("Peek-a-boo") and continue inventing throughout childhood. Figuring out a strategy for winning at *nim,* for example, probably mankind's oldest mathematical game and still played by children around the world, possibly motivated Pythagoras to begin the study of number theory. This, in turn, generated the discipline of mathematics, a parent of all sciences.

Other evidence supporting the notion that it is open-minded children, rather than adults, who invent the pillars of civilization comes from the study of communication, where researchers have found that children are the inventors of grammar and syntax (Matt Ridley, 1999, 2003). And since nearly all babies have perfect pitch and few adults do, inferential reasoning suggests that it is very young children imitating bird songs and other natural sounds who might have initiated the first steps on the long road toward formal music.

This book does not present a case for the revolutionary idea that children may be one of the inventors of civilization. However, the evidence is compelling that the rise and fall of civilizations is related to the quality of parenting within cultures, although this fact, and the role of children in society, are largely overlooked by both scholars and the general public. The eminent Harvard psychoanalyst, Erik Erikson, wrote ". . . we are also forced to recognize a universal blind spot in the makers and interpreters of history: they ignore the fateful function of childhood in the fabric of society."[1]

With the weakening of societal institutions, families are under great stress. The traditional support structures for parents, typically extended families and villages, as Dr. T. Barry Brazelton pointed out, have been greatly weakened or are no longer available to most families.

The parents' job is further complicated by conflicting advice, contradictory cultural expectations, and the absence of a common philosophical foundation from which problems associated with raising children can be solved. Exacerbating the child rearing task is the reality that most schools teach very little about parenting, and most religious institutions today give inadequate instruction in child development. Thus, most intending parents do not fully appreciate the breadth of knowledge, skills, and the commitment required to raise children successfully.

The ancient models of the successful family have faded in all cultures. Therefore *married couples must create their own new vision of good parenting, guided by the best practices from tradition and the best information from modern science.* Such new images will be motivating to young couples and will reinforce their necessary commitment to become good parents. From their new version of the ideal family will come well-adjusted children who are confident, responsive, emotionally balanced, and who will see the world as fundamentally good.

The authors designed this book to help parents focus on what is universally considered to be the most critical stage in a child's development: pre-

---

1.   Erikson (1963), p. 404.

natal to three years. It is in this sensitive period that the child explores the full range of his or her emotions, all of which must be trained primarily by the child itself, but with the assistance of attentive parents. It is also in this stage that the seeds of the intellect are planted and often begin to flower.

The book opens with some general principles that parents may use in establishing a successful marriage and home. It follows with specific suggestions that the couple will want to consider prior to conception. The book continues with recommendations for parents during and immediately after birth, and provides guidance to new parents for the first three years of the child's life.

From selecting a mate and physical preparation for pregnancy to natural childbirth, breast-feeding, early-childhood education, and moral instruction, parenting must be revolutionized in this new millennium. Intending parents must seek out the best time-tested traditions from all cultures, plus relevant scientific research findings from all disciplines, particularly medicine, child development, sociology, psychology, education, and nutrition. Expectant and committed parents, armed with traditional knowledge, up-to-date research findings, plus their own intuition, will be confident that they have all the guidance they need to raise citizens well-equipped for the ever-changing future.

This book is not encyclopedic, and does not go beyond early childhood. It does not detail the hour-by-hour routines of baby care or chronicle the predictable and almost infinite number of stages that every child traverses. It offers few "prescriptions" to prevent or treat the dozens of illnesses, accidents and disabilities that children suffer, except, for example, breast-feeding, which prevents or mitigates many infectious diseases. Wise parents will browse their libraries, bookstores and the web and keep a few basic references handy from the prenatal period on. Parents should also schedule routine consultations with a competent pediatrician to address problems before they become serious and to assuage their normal anxieties. To assist parents in their general education we highlight in our reference list some of the most important books dealing with the wider range of issues and problems that every competent parent will want to master.

And master those issues they must. All parents, at the close of their lives, invariably look back and ask of themselves, "Did I do a good job as a parent?" Every book on parenting, including this one, seeks to enable each parent to answer, "Yes."

The Universe is orderly,
therefore, it is comprehensible.

–Albert Einstein

Part I
Some General Principles

1

OBEY THE LAWS OF THE UNIVERSE

STUDIES OF THE LIVES of great scientists reveal that nearly all of them grew up in homes that taught them in thousands of ways that there are laws in the universe and that those laws are to be respected.[2]

This principle seems, at once, both obvious and hidden. And the teaching of the principle that the universe is orderly is one of the most important goals and outcomes of successful parenting.

Obviously, there are not two sets of laws operating in our universe,

Figure 1. Einstein proposed that the universe is comprehensible to all humans because the universe is orderly, structured under the rule of law.

one for wise men and women and another for the heedless. Over the long run, all the fundamental laws of nature must operate fairly and justly upon everyone. No one can really break the law of gravity, for example. The child who fails to learn to respect gravity may one day break his leg, but not that law. The laws of the universe, apparently, are self-enforcing.

The principle that the universal laws are self-enforcing seems to apply to individuals, to families, to tribes, to nations, and even to mankind as a whole. The automobile driver who habitually exceeds the speed limits will one day wind up in the hospital or in the morgue. The family that violates the laws of hygiene or nutrition will always be unhealthy, sickly. The tribe that refuses to obey the social laws of cooperation will nearly always lag behind its more cooperative neighbors. The nation that makes a habit of rewarding or electing dishonest men over honest men and women will simply reap more dishonest men who, for their own selfish gains, will lead their nation into bankruptcy.

The laws of the universe appear also to be self-rewarding: families that are frugal or save at a higher rate, e.g., the Jewish, the Italian, the Japanese, the Korean, prosper; the tribes that husband their natural resources, their cattle, and their forests nearly always have a higher standard of living than their neighbors who splurge or who are careless with their natural endowments. The nations that train well and support their farmers will not only be bountiful providers to their own citizens, but they will also earn a position to be benefactors of other nations as well. Israel, once a desert land, exports fruit to Turkey and Europe. America saved much of world from famine following two world wars. While these generalizations do not always hold over the short term, they appear axiomatic over the long term. The bankruptcy of nations and families can be attributed, in part, to our failure to teach these "common sense" observations to our children when the children are young and impressionable. In the world of the future each child is a full citizen, responsible, in part, for the behavior of her family, her tribe, her nation.

Parents who teach this most fundamental principle of the universe, that is, that ours is a universe of law and not of caprice or whim, are preparing their child to respond wisely to an orderly, but ever-changing, universe. In our travels to more than 50 nations, this attitude toward the laws of the universe seems to distinguish the achieving societies from the non-achiev-

---

2.   We are indebted to several researchers for bringing this powerful observation to the notice of the world. Among those offering compelling evidence for this assertion are Harvard psychologist Anne Roe, who studied 64 of America's most respected scientists, 20 biologists, 10 experimental physicists, 12 theoretical physicists, 14 psychologists and 8 anthropologists. These 64 scientists were nominated as "most respected" by their peers, members of the National Academy of Science. David C. McClelland analyzed several contemporary and historic societies, including pre-and post-Columbus Spain, pre- and post-Industrial Revolution Scotland and England, as well as the United States; and Everett C. Hagan who studied Japanese, Burmese, Turk, and other achieving and non-achieving societies. We recommend the basic books of all three of these pioneering scholars: Anne Roe, *The Making of a Scientist*, New York: Dodd, Mead, 1953. David C. McClelland, *The Achieving Society*, Princeton: Van Nostrand, 1961. Everett C. Hagan, *On the Theory of Social Change*, Homewood, Ill.: The Dorsey Press, 1962.

ing societies. Economic and social backwardness then is explained by low achievement drives, a mind-set that good parenting changes.[3]

Children who have been taught to be law-abiding consciously or unconsciously look for that principle in the operation of all things. When they discover that expected order, they can then use that knowledge to master their part of the universe. They will know when to plant their fruit trees, or which fertilizer to use, or when to purify their drinking water, or how to invest their savings, or which career to pursue, when to be strict with their children, and when to be liberal. In short, people who acquire a sense of order and a sense of how to harmonize their behavior with the order of nature are learning how to be intelligent in a universe that demands intelligence.

Such well-organized people will have learned in childhood, from the most significant people in their lives – their parents – the basic principle that will enable them to meet the challenges of life with confidence: the orderly person attracts success, the world is intolerant of the disorderly.

---

3.   The most comprehensive study of the achievement drive across cultures and across time is by Harvard social psychologist David C. McClelland, 1961.

2

MAKE THE HOME ORDERLY

IN THE PHYSICAL SCIENCES (astronomy, chemistry, geology, meteorology, physics), "law" and "order" are almost synonymous. Consider these examples. The "law" of gravity describes how large masses of matter seem to attract each other in a mathematically predictable or orderly way. Bode's Law describes and predicts how the planets arrange themselves in a harmonic or orderly set of concentric ellipses around their sun. The distances are not equal but the distances are mathematically predictable and conform to a discoverable order or law.

Figure 2. *All developmental psychologists agree that the child goes through several stages of development. One of the most pronounced stages, occurring around the age of 20-24 months, is the love of order.*

Behavioral scientists studying human growth and development, see "law" and "order" as sharing a common set of roots in the infant's mind. The newborn appears ready to want to learn both at birth, with her questioning eyes, "Where is that light coming from?" "That sound has a source," the infant seems to say, "What is that source?" Indeed, as Dr. Maria Montessori pointed out, at certain stages the infant seems to demand answers to these and hundreds of other questions, implying a built-in sense that the universe must be explicable, obeying laws and behaving in an orderly fashion!

Law and order mean almost the same thing in describing the cosmos. And, law and order mean almost the same thing in describing the infant's mental evolution.

Every parent must be sensitive to this basic fact of infant development. Every parent must find ways to let his or her child discover the same understanding that Einstein voiced: "The universe is orderly, therefore it is comprehensible." Einstein was, in effect, arguing that the universe is understandable by any normal or sane human mind. Or, in the words of the eminent ecologist, Gregory Bateson, there is a unity between mind and nature.[4]

How do parents teach this fundamental attitude toward the universe? Here are some of the most common ways:

— In most homes around the world, a predictable pattern is presented to the child: breakfast at seven o'clock; lunch at noon; dinner at six; a family hour at seven.

— Many villages set aside a day of the week for washing clothes, another day for going to market, another day for worship, another day for community work projects, another day for sports and games, etc.

— In most parts of the world, very united families set aside one or more days of the year for reunions and all members are expected to gather for certain festive or ceremonial occasions.

— In some urban neighborhoods, the youngsters will be expected to have music or dance or art lessons in the afternoons.

— In some homes, every tool's place is marked; every book has its place on a shelf; every kitchen utensil has its drawer.[5]

All cultures establish and, to varying degrees, enforce, such patterns for several purposes. These patterns give an order to the family and to the society; these patterns furnish a "grammar" whereby the new member can

---

4.   See V. N. Kobayashi, "Mind and Nature: Teaching and Thinking," in William Maxwell (Ed.), *Thinking: The Expanding Frontier*, Philadelphia: The Franklin Institute Press, 1983. Kobayashi writes, "Nature is not perceived directly, but through the lens of the human mind, as influenced and shaped by our purposes and our cultures."

5.   The late Julia Child's model kitchen on display at the Smithsonian in Washington, D.C., illustrates this point. Mr. Child drew outlines to indicate where each pot and pan visibly belonged.

learn the social language of his or her culture. Such patterns teach the child that life – or that part of life that the infant sees – does, in fact, have meaning.

Sociologists call the training of children to understand and to accept such social conventions "socialization," the preparation of the child to participate, without handicap and with confidence, in the life of the culture.

The training of a child to respect orderliness is emphasized because our reading of the lives of the really great and creative men and women reveals that such was the sort of home in which nearly all of them had growing up. The *Encyclopaedia Britannica*, for example, says the following about Mahatma Gandhi: ". . . reared in a morally rigorous environment . . . he soon met prominent social idealists . . . and was shocked at racial discrimination." In the life of Gandhi a chain of effects is suggested: Gandhi was trained by his parents and by his parents' mentors to see the universe as socially and morally orderly. When that perception was united with an enlightened idealism, the result was a moral repugnance at seeing one human violate the dignity of another.

For Einstein, a different problem of "order" in the universe presented itself. The orbit of the planet Mercury seemed chaotic, to be obeying no known laws. Einstein pondered the fact that Newton's "Law of Gravity" did not seem to be powerful enough to keep Mercury in its "proper" orbit. Mercury, Einstein thought, could not really disobey a law of nature. This had to mean that Mercury's apparently confusing or aberrant motion was a result of its following some law other than Newton's. Nature is not lawless, he reasoned. These and similar meditations led Einstein to give birth to the Theory of Relativity, a set of laws more powerful than those discovered by Newton.

It is not the case that Mercury's mass was indifferent to or defied the mass of the Sun. The "law" or "theory" that Einstein discovered was that Mercury was responding "religiously" to the *shape* of space, not merely to the mass of the sun. Einstein's insight was that space exerted an influence, due in part, to its proximity to the Sun. In Newton's universe, space had no shape and, therefore, no influence. Einstein gave the world a fuller picture of space, time, and matter because he knew that there had to be laws underlying the movement of every body, every atom, in space. He knew that no planet, no atom, is above the law.

Similarly, the Wright brothers did not desire to break the law of gravity when they decided to invent powered aviation. They were simply searching for ways of understanding the laws that enabled birds to fly, laws that were not in conflict with Newton's law of gravity.

Thus, modern aviation, Gandhi's non-violent ideas and Einstein's theories of the universe proceed from the same basic source: a respect, even love, for "Law and Order." This respect or love is a seed planted in the earliest days of a child's life and produces a disciplined human mind that, in turn, produces ideas, which advance the human race.

When Massachusetts Institute of Technology professor Everett C. Hagan said that "the creative individual has a sense that the world is orderly" he might have had in mind the research study of Anne Roe. Roe quotes one of her distinguished research subjects: "In a large family I learned to read before I went to school . . . About the time I went to high school we moved to a farm and father wanted the farm to run scientifically . . . We would plant a plot of this and a plot of that and keep records of it."[6]

The personality with high achievement motivation nearly always scores high on these two qualities: a love of order and a love of experimenting.

Children begin experimenting from the time they are born to discover the laws of nature and of man. Every experiment, whether of man, of child, or of infant, represents a hope that some higher or previously undiscovered order or law will be found. Wise parents, therefore, encourage the child to experiment, to try to discover for itself the underlying order holding the universe together.

On the one hand parents must uphold an order and regularity in the home and, on the other hand, they must allow the child the freedom to discover, to seek new explanations for the ways things behave, to experiment.

The orderly home, then, is the beginning of the scientific intellect *and* the source of the social conscience.

---

6.   Anne Roe, *The Making of a Scientist*, New York: Dodd, Mead, 1953 (p. 75). Anne Roe's method of study was to interview in great detail her subjects. What was surprising at that time, more than 50 years ago, was the unusual candor about their private and personal lives that those men evinced. It was as if they wanted everyone to know the secrets of their success.

3

SHOWER THE CHILD WITH LOVE

AT CERTAIN STAGES, the greatest joy of a child is to be alone with one of the parents. The child's preference oscillates between mother and father. Sensitive parents must be aware of this fact and not become jealous or angry. These oscillations begin about 42 days after birth when the infant is ready to fall in love with the father and end by age five or six when the child will have incorporated both mother and father into his/her psyche, ideally as one.[7, 8]

The great and creative individuals of history, and of our time, were nearly always reared in homes of "law and order." Perhaps even more importantly, they were also raised in homes with abundant love and affection. The difference that a loving home makes is strikingly evident, not only in the creative or intellectual abilities of a child, but also in the child's total personality. After all, the creative or intellectual abilities alone do not

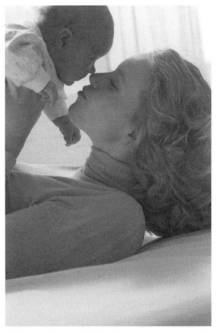

Figure 3. All infants expect to be loved, to have all of their basic needs met immediately. Burton White, for many years the child-development researcher at Harvard University, argued that it is impossible to spoil a child within the first six months.

determine a child's ultimate success or status in life. Many other personality variables operate as well.

Observing children in any culture is instructive. And having lived and worked in various cultural regions of the world, we are in a position to compare personalities of children from various child rearing styles or traditions. Although children everywhere manifest Dr. Maria Montessori's description, we think we were enabled to better appreciate part of the secret of a child's special attractiveness after observing children in Northeast Asia, West Africa, Oceania, as well as in Europe and the United States.

But first let us summarize, in Montessori's words, the timeless principles that must characterize adult-child relationships in any healthy society:

> The special object of a child's affection is the adult. He receives from the adult the material help he needs for his self-development. For the child, the adult is a kind of venerable being. From his lips, as from a spring, he draws the words he must learn and so, burning with love, an adult should carefully weigh all the words he speaks to him . . .

> It is really the child who loves, who wants to feel an adult near him, and who delights in attracting attention to himself. (pp. 104 - 5)[9]

---

7.   Mary Ainsworth is the psychologist who pioneered the study of infant attachment or bonding. Born in Ohio, she moved to Canada as a teen-ager and earned her doctorate at the University of Toronto. Her research studies were conducted in Uganda, Britain, Baltimore and elsewhere. Ainsworth's studies of "strange situation" behavior by children explained why some children are more adaptable to new experiences. Mothers who are consistently present to respond to their children's discoveries and problems are preparing their children to face many types of life crises with greater confidence, she found. For a summary of Mary Ainsworth's research studies see William Crain (2005).

8.   The infant bonds first with the mother. Then after about 42 days "the social smile" emerges. We refer to this milestone as the infant's desire to bond with the father, then later to a larger social circle. (See Gordon W. Allport, 1954.) The social smile is wide, involves nearly all facial muscles and is focussed upon a particular person. In our view, the ideal object of this smile is the father.

9.   Maria Montessori, *The Secret of Childhood.* (M. Joseph Costello, S.J., Tr.) New York: Ballantine Books, 1974.

It seems to us that two powerful forces must operate in the evolving mind of every child if that child is to be truly civilized, if the child is to conquer his own barbaric impulses. One force is seen as law and order, an idea, no doubt very vague at first, that the universe is ruled by cause and effect relationships, that every event is caused and that every act has consequences. In the Sanskrit language that force or law is called *Karma*. Karma expresses in one word that universal law, that concept that all acts are rewarded or punished, the concept that the universe must always remain in balance, in harmony; that no one can do wrong and get away with it.

The other and equally powerful force is love. Rarely, very rarely, has one who was greatly loved by both mother and father throughout the early years of life lost his/her sanity. Every wise book that discusses this topic emphasizes the same thing. Most spiritual traditions and the books of such leading psychologists as Alfred Adler or Carl Jung or Eric Erikson all stress the imperative that the human child requires enormous quantities of love. Indeed, there appears to be a moral law of the universe that a child should not come into being unless both mother and father are present to protect it and to love it.[10]

How does one manifest this love for such a helpless creature as the newborn child? Obviously, there will be countless ways to translate the abstract concept of love into "deeds of respect." To the ancient and chiefly class of Fijians, a new baby was truly a blessed event. The Fijians manifested their love for the newborn by never letting it out of someone's arms. The infant was cuddled constantly for at least three weeks following birth.[11] To the newborn, love is close skin-to-skin contact, close enough to hear or to feel another heartbeat or pulse, close enough to hear or to feel and to learn the basic rhythms of life, the unanxious music of the loving heart. To the newborn, love is constant dry comfort and warmth, readily available mother's milk, the absence of pain, dim lights, modulated sounds, and tender, soft movements.

---

10. Most human societies establish mechanisms to ensure that the child will always have at least two parents. For example, the Catholics created the "godfather" and "godmother" concept. In the unwritten codes of the Hausas of West Africa, the child's father's father serves as a second father. In Samoa that father back-up role is fulfilled by the mother's older brother.

In many villages of the world, especially in the Pacific and in parts of Africa, even in this insensitive age, there are still taboos against loud sounds near the newborn.

For a child around 42 days old, love is a father whose face lights up at the sight of that child. Several different kinds of experiments have shown that as the child develops, it seems to "demand," almost as if by right, the presence of another adult, someone other than the mother; someone with a deeper or more masculine voice, another kind of face. A child feels love if its presence brings a warm smile to the face of the father. At another stage in its development – the ancient Koreans fixed this stage as occurring at 100 days after birth – the child requires a grandmother's love, or the love of an aunt or of an uncle, each of which takes on a different form, forms which are very different from the love of the mother and father.

A child needs all of these different kinds of love. The analogy is made between the human infant and a tomato seedling. The new tomato plant needs several different kinds of minerals, and varying amounts of sunlight if it is to develop to its full ripeness and taste. Iron is not enough. A mother's love, while necessary, is not sufficient.

The issue of spoiling the child in its early days need not arise. None of the child's wants are dangerous – either to it or to the family. The child's wants are simple and basic. The child wants closeness to another human; it wants to be dry and comfortable; to have warm human milk; freedom from pain; and a few other harmless desires. How can fulfilling such simple, innocent wants be interpreted as "spoiling" the child? Later on, if the child wants to play with matches or if it manifests unreasoning jealousy of

---

11.   One of the authors was having lunch one day in downtown Suva, Fiji, with the Chief of Staff of the Fijian Army, Colonel Epeli Nailatikau. "How are things at home?", the author asked. "Terrible," the young colonel answered with a mixed emotions smile. "They have thrown me out." "Who is they?" the author asked. "My wife's mother and sisters have moved in," he answered. The wife's mother and sisters had not actually thrown the husband out on the street. But the entire household routine and sleeping patterns had to be radically changed in preparation for the birth and customary 21-day caring period in which this high-born baby would have "24/7", around the clock, skin-to-skin care by female relatives of the mother. Perhaps the confidence gained by such babies explains why the Fijian Army is generally the first military unit called by the United Nations for peace-keeping duties around the world. Tall, strong, self-assured, the Fijian soldiers not only are welcomed everywhere, they have an enviable record of not attracting hostility wherever they go.

a sibling, then allowing the child the full play of its passions would be to spoil it. But in its early days and weeks of life, the issue of spoiling the child is not a concern.

In the Japanese culture, almost every wish of the child is a command, up until about age six. In such a child-loving culture, the child naturally learns the acceptable limits of behavior to become law-abiding.[12]

One of the most painful anxieties to afflict human beings relates to whether one is loved. Perhaps the first question that the newborn asks after birth, in its unschooled but intelligent way, is: "Does the Universe love me?" This is the burning question that every human appears to ask, long before the appearance of speech. That is the question that the great teachers from Moses to Plato asked – and answered.

One of the premier goals of parent education is to *train* parents how to answer that profound question affirmatively, in all contingencies, to every newborn.

When "law and order" are enthroned in the child's mind, that mind will have stability. When love is enthroned in the child's heart, there will be strength. Great souls have both.

These are the two greatest gifts from one's parents: a sense that the universe operates within systems of laws, and a deep and unconscious certitude that one is loved.

---

12. Is this one reason why Japan has one of the lowest crime rates in the world? That is, the Japanese person, having been well-nurtured in childhood, is more inclined to accept and obey society's rules.

4

ALLOW THE CHILD INDEPENDENCE

ONE OF THE MOST important books of the twentieth century is David C. McClelland's *The Achieving Society*[13] which represents a search for answers to one of the most perplexing problems facing social scientists: why is it

---

13. McClelland's book is a refinement and a recasting, with the benefit of more than seven decades of social science research, of the great sociological classic by Max Weber, *The Protestant Ethic and the Rise of Capitalism*. Weber's argument, over-simplified for the sake of brevity, is that Western European Civilization excelled all others due to a Protestant Ethic instilled into the European cultures by preachers and writers such as John Calvin and John Bunyon. Calvin's and Bunyon's exhortations to improve the world were accepted and transmitted by parents to their children while the children were young.

McClelland writes, "The mothers of the (low achievers) reported more restrictions; they did not want their sons to play with children not approved by the parents, nor did they want them to make important decisions by themselves. The picture here is reasonably clear. The mothers of the sons with high (need for) achievement have set higher standards for their sons; they expect self-reliance and mastery at an earlier age. That is, the Winterbottom study suggests a psychological means by which the historical development described by Weber may have come about. The Protestant Reformation might have led to earlier independence and mastery training, which led to greater (need for) achievement which, in turn, led to the rise of modern capitalism . . . Certainly, Weber's description of the kind of personality type which the Protestant Reformation produced is startlingly similar to the picture we have drawn of a person with high achievement motivation." (McClelland, 1966, p. 47.)

Neither Weber nor McClelland said that such achievement motivation is exclusive to Western Civilization. The drive to improve the world exists everywhere at all times, but in varying degrees. That motivation reached critical mass in China 5,000, 2,000 and 1,000 years ago and reached a critical mass in the Islamic world in the ninth century, A.D. That critical mass seems now to be on the threshold of being universal.

that very few societies achieve a measure of greatness while the vast majority do not? What are the secrets of "an ever-advancing civilization?"[14]

After studying that societal question, McClelland erects a theory, the most important pillar of which is the mother-child interactions. One of his most persuasive pieces of evidence came from a study regarding the amount of independence training *given to* or *allowed* infants and young children by their mothers.

Figure 4. "Bye, Mom, I'm on my own." Maria Montessori, in her book "The Absorbent Mind", taught that the strongest drive in the child is the independence drive.

The essence of the study cited by McClelland was that the individuals who would later, in maturity, be identified as high-achievers were given more independence as infants than were their low-achieving cohorts.

Infants begin to manifest a need for independence from birth – or earlier. For example, once having learned how to find the mother's nipple – usually in about six to 15 seconds if hungry and not under stress – the infant shows anger if the mother insistently guides his head to the nipple in later feedings. The infant wants to find the nipple for himself. One of the authors has observed, particularly in West Africa, that some infants want to find it for themselves even on the first feeding!

Sensitive mothers soon notice such early independence motivations in their infants and allow the newborn to feed itself from then on.

The infant's "cycle of independence" continually re-asserts itself. At eight months, the child will literally demand the spoon or literally demand the

14. By "greatness" McClelland meant societies that encourage high achievement drives in citizens and produce a large number of such persons, although McClelland and other social psychologists emphasized that the social climate that produces the achievement drive is supported by a strong spiritual base. That is, the two are inseparable.

right to feed itself. In many instances the infant will refuse to take its food from mother, even if hungry. At times, and the times will vary in frequency and intensity from individual to individual, the drive for independence is stronger than the so-called hunger drive.

The mothers of such men and women as Thomas Edison or Marie Curie understood this need for independence and wisely adjusted their mothering behavior to accommodate it. That is, the mothers of high-achievers do not thwart that independence motivation; rather, they encourage it.

If one watches a child after 8 months, one sees many recurring cycles of the drive for independence – alternating with the contrary need for affiliation; for dependence. At around age two years, the child will try to run as far as possible from mother and father in a park. The child will play a game of "independence" that it thinks it has invented. It will stray as far as its tolerance for the thought of being "lost" will allow. The child will "play" or "experiment" with the contradictory emotions of "security" and "independence", balancing them in its mind. He discovers that both emotions are exquisite and both are necessary.

Successful parents somehow learn – and we know of no definitive studies that tell us *how* they learn this – to balance their interactions with the child so that it is the *child*, not the *parents*, who determines when the parents should allow the child freedom and when to draw the child away from freedom and toward imitative and other dependent behaviors.

But if the parents frustrate or discourage the child's naturally recurring "cycle of independence," they will hinder the development of those important skills associated with discovering new things; they will be thwarting the development of those skills we find in the high-achieving individuals.

Unless the mind has both the security of dependence and the confidence of independence, it is unlikely to train itself to become successful either in the world of the intellect or in the world of the imagination or entreprenurship.[15]

---

15. David McClelland (1961) postulated that the frequency and intensity of individuals' independence drive (entrepreneurial spirit) explains the rise of high civilizations, and the relative lack of such a drive helps to explain why many parts of the world lag behind other nations in social and economic development.

5

TEACH YOUR CHILD JUSTICE

JUSTICE IS NOT natural. One cannot find in nature any models of the human or divine concept of justice. Mankind must express thanks to the Greeks, particularly to Socrates and Plato[16] and to Confucius, for articulating "Justice" as one of the goals of our social evolution. No society that we know of has yet established that exalted virtue. But, fortunately, all humans can imagine a society where justice reigns. This is another paradox of human nature. We have never seen justice, but we can imagine its existence.

We realize that this philosophical abstraction, that justice exists within the mind of an individual, is difficult to prove and, perhaps, has reality only on some intuitive level. Hagan, in analyzing Japan's sudden emergence as a world power, noted something operating in that culture akin to what we are trying to say: "The doctrine emerged that one's family, one's lord (chief), one's country, and the Gods had conferred on one a blessing infinite in extent by bringing one into being, rearing one, and giving one the opportunity to live. One (therefore) must recognize the infinite obligation one owes in return and work all one's life to repay it."[17] Thus Hagan found in the Japanese culture a

Figure 5. Plato taught that justice is learned in fair play, therefore, the ideal curriculum for all children includes a wide variety of games.

"Puritan" ethos almost identical to that in parts of the West. That puritan ethos – which among other things says that we work hard out of gratitude, not guilt – exists to some extent in all human cultures. The establishment of that belief is a major milestone in achieving justice. The seed of that belief is planted in early childhood.

Few great men and women were unjust. Most great persons, it seems to us from our sampling of important biographies, possess a very high ethical value system. They were trained by their parents and teachers to see the world as potentially fair. In the same spirit as the hero of Bunyon's *Pilgrim's Progress*[18] they see themselves as co-workers with a divine force to improve the universe. They wish to reduce illness or suffering, create wealth, raise the general standard of living, help people to communicate better, to be happier, to know more, to appreciate life.

How do parents instill in their child this rare virtue? When one visits a school in most parts of the world, one usually notices the bright and cheerful children first. But close, or more extended, observation will present one with the "mean" child, the child who "picks on" crippled children or darker-skinned children; the bully, the little bigot. One then asks, "Will nature bestow her secrets upon that child whose psyche already reflects narrow-mindedness?" Narrow-mindedness is more than a figure of speech. It is not entirely a metaphor. The word expresses a fact. Noble ideas have trouble entering narrow minds. Parents must avoid conditioning their child to be narrow-minded. That is, children must be taught that the universe and nature are generous, bountiful, and expansive.

---

16. Some readers of this manuscript protested that Plato, a leading member of the Greek aristocracy, was not a "justice seeker" since he believed in somewhat rigid social hierarchies and appeared to disdain democracy. Others have argued that Jefferson, being a slave owner, had no license to write that, "We hold these truths to be self-evident, that all man are created equal . . .". In defense of Plato and Jefferson we propose that those men reflected, and were restrained by, their times and cultures, but also transcended their times and cultures in some important ways. Can we forgive them for being less than perfect? We think we must, since they pointed out to us not only the possibility of justice but, in fact, suggested ways to achieve it.

17. Everett C. Hagan, *On the Theory of Social Change*. Homewood, Illinois: The Dorsey Press. 1962.

18. Bunyan, John (1628-1688), *Pilgrim's Progress*, Grand Rapids, MI: Christian Classics Ethereal Library. This book was required reading for all educated people in Britain and the United States in the 19th and early 20th centuries.

When parents speak disparagingly of other ethnic or national groups they condition their children to be bigots and condemn them to a life less than their full potential. The snob rarely moves mankind a notch forward. Indeed, the snob, the small-minded, retard man's growth.

Another place to observe the unjust person is in prisons. In teaching courses in adolescent psychology, one of the authors asks his university students to interview prisoners and ask questions about their early life and the child rearing practices under which they were raised. A typical pattern emerges. The prisoner inflicted an injustice upon someone because, in effect, he was conditioned as a child to expect injustice. Disputes were settled by violence. The home was a place of pain.

Teaching the child justice has to be a conscious and deliberate pattern of family behavior. The most fundamental place for the teaching of that noble virtue is the home.[19]

---

19. Chapter 40 takes a brief look at the idea of justice from a different perspective.

6

TEACH YOUR CHILD TO THINK

EVERY TIME A CHILD solves one problem, he or she opens the door to solving dozens, if not hundreds, of similar problems. Therefore, one definition of intelligence is the ability to solve unsolved and unanticipated problems.

To solve a problem, one needs to think. Most religions and philosophies have concluded that it is the fate of mankind to be presented with increasingly difficult challenges. The Book of Job is but one example. The logical implication, which has escaped most leaders of religions and teachers of culture, is that every child must be taught to think – to think independently.

Figure 6. Maria Montessori demonstrated that children learn about 60 times faster than adults. Their brains are active all the time, even in sleep. A secret of superior parenting is to expose the child to a huge variety of new learning experiences in an appropriate sequence and at the right time, but not to over-stimulate the child. Montessori advised taking cues from the child. Your child will guide you in what she or he is ready to learn.

The realm of creative thinking, then, describes the next great frontier that the human species is compelled to explore if we are to continue to evolve, if we are to experience the joy of living successfully.

This book focuses on facilitating one's child to develop his or her intelligence, with intelligence being defined as the skillful use of a large repertory of thinking techniques. The implication of the above problem-centered universe idea is that every member of the human species is challenged continuously to solve problems and create something new. This means that every child is inherently intelligent. But that intelligence must be cultivated in order to reach the stage that Erik Erikson named "Generativity vs. Stagnation," and that Maslow placed at the peak of his "Hierarchy of Needs" as "Self Actualization."[20]

The idea that each child is capable of creating something new was particularly conveyed by Socrates and his intellectual descendants. Beginning in the 19th century, that idea began to be asserted by an increasing number of scientists as well.

Thus, the obvious question arises: how do parents facilitate their child's becoming intelligent, so that he or she will have the mental power to overcome the obstacles that will be thrown in his or her way, and to bring into being his or her noble ideas?

All 50 chapters of this book, in effect, respond to that question. Here are eight opening suggestions:

1) *New or intending parents should take one of Edward de Bono's courses on thinking* so as to hone their own thinking skills and become aware of the many ways that ordinary minds may become creative minds. Edward de Bono's courses[21] are available via the web at www.edwarddebono.com/family.

Professor de Bono makes the point that schools do a fair to good job of teaching *literacy* and *numeracy* (facility with words and numbers), but do a very inadequate job teaching what he calls "*operancy*" (how to do things) and *thinking skills*. The inference is that the parents must step in and teach all those skills, particularly the latter two.

2) The parents should *read at least one of Professor Edward de Bono's 68 books on thinking*. We list five of them here.

   a) *Six Thinking Hats*, Boston: Little, Brown and Company, 1985.
   b) *de Bono's Thinking Course*, New York: Facts on File, 1994.

---

20. Erikson (1950) and Maslow (1968) both believed that the stage of creativity they described is attainable by everyone and is not exclusive to geniuses.

21. The world owes a great debt of gratitude to Edward de Bono for defining intelligence as the ability to solve new and unpredicted problems and for venturing the next logical step, which is developing programs to train adults and children in the specific skills of creative thinking, or problem-solving.

c) *Teach Your Child How to Think*, London: Penguin. 1993.

d) *Serious Creativity*, Perfection Learning, New York: Harper Business, 1992.

e) *Children Solve Problems*. London: Viking Penguin. 1974.

3) *Parents should familiarize their children with intelligence tests and other methods of assessing mental competence.* The child should grow to expect such regular mental checkups as essential as regular physical checkups. Nearly all first-rate universities and most "high-tech" firms screen applicants with some form of intelligence test. (Test anxiety can be managed or prevented by familiarity.) IQ tests are to the mind what a gymnasium is to the body. The mental alertness assessment given at birth, the Apgar Test, is a more recent and a very simple mental assessment instrument, like an IQ test, and is vitally necessary. The Apgar Test measures five functions each of which is given a score from 0 to 2. Thus the true function of IQ tests is to find out as early as possible if there are brain function problems so that those problems can be corrected immediately. In addition to that function, IQ tests for children also stretch the mind and alert the child as to what he or she should know and what reasoning skills he or she is expected to have. We agree with administering the Apgar Test and other IQ tests such as the Stanford-Binet and the Peabody Picture Vocabulary Test, which tell the pediatrician and the parents if development is on schedule. Obviously, if development is not on schedule, diagnosis and remediation are strongly urged.

For monthly mental check-up tests from birth to age six, we suggest the Ames/Gesell reference below (page 158). We recommend that the parents select five or 10 items corresponding to their child's age from the Ames book once per month to see how well their baby is progressing (Ames, 1979, or any subsequent revision). Such a routine is much more scientific than comparing one's baby to a cousin or to a neighbor's baby. Such monthly confirmations are inspiring and will motivate excellent parents to be even better parents.

4) We recommend from age 5½ to 15 years, "*Inventive Quotient: The Child's First Course in Logical Reasoning*," by William Maxwell and Larry Sanford (www.inventivequotient.com). The first of four CDs contains 2,400 thinking skills test items that are randomly presented to the child at each monthly testing. After answering 25 questions, the child is given an intelligence score range. The score is never a single number, since

intelligence scores, like physical-fitness scores, fluctuate widely. The CD also contains daily mental exercises designed to challenge all parts of the brain. These mentally challenging exercises are recommended for about seven minutes per day.

5) Since the mother and the father are inventive, *we urge the parents to create some unique activities* on a regular basis that will cultivate their child's mind. For example, the Scots invented "The Parenting Hour," a period after dinner, after all the chores were done, in which the family read together, played parlor games, made music; and discussed "life 101."[22]

6) *Observe other intelligent parents as they deal with their children.*[23]

7) One of the oldest ways that highly successful parents teach their children to be discerning and analytical is by *encouraging the child to collect things.* Collecting implies ordering and understanding the value or historical or geographic context of the item being collected. Franklin Delano Roosevelt was one of the best known stamp-collectors and delighted in exhibiting his collections to visitors, even state visitors.

---

22. David McClelland at Harvard (1961) and Everett Hagan at MIT (1962) proposed a connection between the Scots' highly innovative "Parenting Hour" during the late 1600s and early 1700s and the emergence of the Industrial Revolution in the United Kingdom.

23. One of the authors had lunch with a successful father and psycho-therapist, who told an inspiring story of how he taught his children important problem-solving skills. One of the stories validates the advice to "Keep the Home Orderly." About once per month, Stephen Lankton said, he would play a "What has Changed?" game with his children. The father and the three children would go into the room of one of the children and the father would say, "Take a careful look around the room. After you have noticed where everything is and how it is ordered, you will leave the room. Then I will move six things. You will return to the room and your task is to discover which six things I moved. Often, Mr. Lankton said, when the child came back into the room he or she would discover something out of order that the father had not moved. The child then would say something like, "This music box is not squared on the bureau." And the child would square the music box, or whatever. Typically, the child would find those six items that the father had moved. Then, the roles would be reversed. The father would leave the room after taking a good look at it and the child would move six things. The father's task, of course, was to discover what had been re-arranged or moved. Mr. Lankton reported that when visitors came into his home, they were always surprised at how orderly the children's rooms were. The children took pride in their order. The middle child graduated with highest honors from Georgia Tech in robotics. The other two children are similarly successful.

Collecting coins, stones, doll clothing, sea shells, leaves, berries, nuts, are similarly fascinating hobbies for a large number of children and often give clues as to the child's possible "True Calling."

8) Gordon Dryden of New Zealand, and author of *The Learning Revolution,* which has sold more than 12,000,000 copies worldwide, cautions Americans that the U.S. educational system is behind other industrialized nations, even though most of the technology sparking the learning revolution was developed in the United States. Dryden therefore advises Americans that *they must be very selective in choosing schools for their children* and not assume that an expensive school is up-to-date in delivering a 21st century education. Dryden's book is now available on the internet at no cost.

In sum, parents facilitate their child's process of learning to think by allowing the child great independence, as was recommended by Montessori and McClelland, and by paying close attention to the child's curious and energetic mind and responding positively, in non-formulaic ways, to that still developing "beautiful mind."

Part II
Some Specific Suggestions to Consider Prior to Conception

7

CHOOSE A MATE WITH HEALTHY GENES

DR. THEODOSIUS DOBZHANSKY'S work on genetics has helped to modify important aspects of Darwin's Theory of Evolution. Among Dobzhansky's ideas is that the (one) human race is still evolving biologically and that human evolution illustrates an element of "conscious decision-making." In mating, for example, evolution is promoted by "outbreeding" (as opposed to "inbreeding").

A few geneticists and eugenicists, such as Sir Francis Galton, Sir Cyril Burt, Prof. Arthur Jensen and others, are convinced that intelligence and many other traits are principally the results of genes that correlate with race. There is, of course, much evidence that mental strength or agility and some other mental traits have a "heritability" component. But where these "experts"

Figure 7. Geneticist Dr. Theodosius Dobzhansky

have erred, we believe, is in going from individual cases, where the evidence is somewhat persuasive, all the way up to enormously large populations, including ethnic groups and nationalities.

The most obvious argument that intelligence is not ethnically determined is that intelligence will vary more *within* ethnic groups than *across* ethnic groups. That is, there is some evidence that in the 15th century, the smartest people in Europe were Italians, Spaniards, and Portuguese. Yet, no one would dispute that those national groups had about as many feeble-minded as the Danes or the Swedes; or that Sweden had almost as many geniuses as Italy. If one averaged the intelligence scores of all of Europe's various ethnic groups, the differences would have been insignificant. Ethnicity or nationality would not be the important variable.

Let us state the case clearly. We believe that intelligence is fairly randomly distributed among all human ethnic groups and that it is as fruitless to try to correlate intelligence with ethnicity as it is pointless to correlate swimming or walking speed with ethnicity. The only variables operating are probably those that can be manipulated. These are the culturally determined factors: physical health, and the variables relating to nurturing, education, and the moral environment.

However, one must be aware that genetic defects occur in all ethnic groups and that each individual human carries some genetic weaknesses. One's statistical chances for finding a mate with complementary genes for one's child *rise* if one marries *outside* one's own genetic pool. In this context, anthropologists define a genetic pool as one's own clan, or a tribal unit of less than ten thousand people.

The simplest way to ensure healthy progeny is to choose a mate from a different genetic pool. If Mr. A, for example, belongs to Tribe M and he chooses a girl, Miss B from Tribe M, the chances will be high that his and her genetic weaknesses will be reinforced in their children. However, if Mr. A chooses a girl, Miss L, from Tribe K, a different genetic pool, the probability of their having the same genetic weakness or defects falls. In the latter case, a very powerful genetic law can then operate: the new individual, the offspring of both, can now "choose" the strongest genes available from *both* parents. There is powerful evidence that given a choice between a "weak" gene and a "strong" gene, pure chance does *not* operate. There is not a 50:50 probability that the new individual will choose the gene of the "weak-eyed" parent, for example. Rather, there is a 90:10 or 80:20 probability that the body of the new individual will choose the gene of the "strong-eyed" parent.[24]

Researchers have observed that in tribes with high levels of inbreeding there seems to be higher levels of certain physical and mental infirmities than would be predicted by chance or by non-genetic factors such as economic levels. That is, where members of the tribe inbreed, one finds higher levels of mental illness and feeble-mindedness as well as incidences of genetically based physical diseases.

Figure 8.   One reason that women are attracted to strong men is the woman's conscious or unconscious awareness that one of the husband's and father's roles is to protect the family. Men have an obligation to remain fit therefore, which also has for the man a survival benefit.

Because there are hundreds of diseases or disabilities that are directly related to genetic defects we believe that genetic counseling will become an integral part of premarital counseling in the future. Well educated young people will see marriage not only as a private matter, but also as an institution established to ensure the welfare of each person and of the human race as a whole.

---

24. One of the most thorough examinations of the "genetics" question was recently completed by Matt Ridley, *Genome: The Autobiography of a Species in 23 Chapters.* New York: HarperCollins Publishers. 1999. The world is indebted to Ridley for clearing up much of the confusion about genetics. In a subsequent book he writes, "My argument in a nutshell is this: the more we lift the lid on the genome (the entire genetic code for mankind), the more vulnerable to experience genes appear to be" (2003, p.4). In other words, genes are not hard immutable deterministic balls, dictating our appearance or behavior. They are living things, frequently full of error, they fight, they "run and hide," they cooperate, they gang up on each other. Genes are often flawed, but they appear to be, like humans, sometimes self-perfecting. Ridley's position is that an individual's behavior or personality is a "blend" of both nature (genetic inputs) and nurture (environment). He argues that some of our behaviors are inherited (or have a genetic base) and do, in fact, fall into the category that biologists call "instinct." Whether we agree or not with the geneticists, a person is well advised to look into the genetic background of one's potential mate. The Chinese, among others, have found it wise to do so for centuries.

8

BE CHASTE BEFORE MARRIAGE

Figure 9. Chastity is appreciated in all cultures. All intending parents should meditate on the advantages of chastity before marriage, preferably in what Freud called the "latency period," before the sexual urges of adolescence set in.

DO VIRGINS MAKE BETTER parents? Both males and females have a *biological* responsibility (and the urges) to reproduce the human race. They have also been assigned, by every society on this planet, a *societal* responsibility as well: to socialize the child, to enculturate the child into its culture, that is, to educate the child on how to participate in the ongoing evolution of his or her culture. Like members of the bird families, the human infant requires double-time care, actually, even more than double-time care initially. The human infant's physical, emotional, educational, and psychological needs are so great that they cannot be met by one parent alone. Are those needs of the infant better met by parents who are tightly bonded or parents who are loosely bonded?

That a child requires at least two parents plus, has not been seriously questioned by any of the 6,000 or so human societies. This need for two parents, at least two, therefore must be accepted as fundamental to the human race. This obvious need further implies that there must be a bonding between the parents so that the child will have, just as little birds have, a social insurance policy.[25] Before the child comes into being it needs strong prior assurance that both mother and father will dedicate themselves to its needs which, physically, psychologically (emotionally and cognitively), are enormous, as the food needs of the baby bird are enormous. The strongest possible insurance policy for the new infant, then, is the degree of commitment between its parents.

We have observed in several major cultural regions of the world that if either of the parents is casual in his or her sexuality, he or she is less likely to be emotionally able to establish a strong bond with the child's other parent. If, on the other hand, both parents are chaste before marriage, and faithful within the marriage, their chances of bonding for life, or at least for the first 15 years of the child's life, will be substantially increased. Sex, besides being a source of physical pleasure for most people, is also a powerful force to help bond two chaste people together in love.

Teen-agers often confuse sex and love. Love and sex, obviously, are not synonyms. However, to some degree, teen-agers such as Romeo and Juliet are right: that first true love, a combination of physical, emotional, and intellectual attraction, is a powerful force with many potentially beautiful consequences. One positive consequence is that both partners and any off-spring of their union will desire that the union last forever. Puccini in another classical teen-age love story, "Turandot" which Puccini adapted for the operatic stage as symbolic of that pure love that chaste people so often manifest, expresses this deeply emotional commitment when Caleb, the princely hero, says of Turandot, the princess heroine of the opera, "Either (I win) Turandot or I die."

Although these classical and romantic ideal love stories are rare in our era, they are still possible. More importantly, such relatively pure love is still valued by virtually all human societies because this ideal has its own rewards. For example, all the great scientists who were studied by Anne Roe were virgins at marriage, except two. And even those two were certainly not promiscuous. Each of those 64 respected scientists fell deeply in love, we can infer, channeled their love in the family, had reasonably happy married lives, and enjoyed the fruits of both worlds: the physical pleasure of a happy union and the intellectual ecstasy of discovering something new about our amazing universe.

---

25. In most bird species the female will not mate until the male has created a nest for the family. The male-female bond remains until the chicks are mature.

Indeed, it would appear from a study of the lives of great scientists that the creative energies function more powerfully if the sexual energies are controlled and disciplined. Erik Erikson, the professor of psychology at Harvard, noticed this correlation. He suggested that one of the factors making for a successful integration of the personality was the degree to which the person successfully "sublimated his libidinal drives." "Sublimate" does not mean, in this context, to repress. It means to *channel*, to defer sexual gratification until one is able to focus on one's mate, to bond permanently to the one opposite pole.

Sex is like electricity. Uninsulated, it wreaks havoc. Insulated and switched on at the right time, sex can "light up" every cell of the body, including the creative cells of the brain.

On the other side of the coin, we have had our students in various parts of the world study inmates of prisons and juvenile-detention centers. The lessons that these university students learn are instructive: while there are several variables operating to produce criminal behavior, in virtually every case, the prison inmate, in describing the climate of his or her home during his or her early years, reports that chastity was not valued. Indeed, in almost every instance, the person in prison had personal knowledge that one or the other of his or her parents were adulterous, and that one or both parents were promiscuous before the prison subject was born.

Culturally, possibly one of the best examples for the advantages of chastity before marriage is the Ibo tribe of southeastern Nigeria, the third largest tribe of that country. In 1920, the literacy rate was estimated to be under three percent; there was not one high school in the entirety of "Ibo-land." By the 1960's the Ibos were excelling the much "older" tribes, the Hausa, who had established Koranic schools for centuries, and the Yoruba who had great cities and advanced international commerce since the sixteenth century, and who had been trading with the Portuguese for 500 years. The Ibos were training over 100 medical doctors per year, were producing four or five times more engineers and scientists as African-Americans who had been "freed" six decades earlier. The striking difference between the Ibos and their neighbors attracted the attention of such scholars as Robert A. Levine, then at Chicago, later at Harvard, who received a large grant from the Carnegie Foundation to study why the Ibos exceeded all their neighbors in Africa on virtually every measure of societal health. Robert A. Levine found several important variables operating. The Ibos, to a degree greater than their neighbors, held chastity before marriage in high esteem.

The sublimation of the sexual drive led to heightened achievement drive and helped the Ibos to dominate all of the university entrance examination results and other measures of intellectual achievement.

The most obvious rewards for chastity before marriage are children who are emotionally secure and healthy within a family system that they perceive as stable and permanent. The prisons of the world, on the other hand, are filled with inmates from unstable unions. The laws of the universe are self-enforcing.

In the social sciences arena, there are few absolutes. Suppose that neither the man nor the woman has been chaste before marriage. Are they doomed to be inadequate parents? Fortunately, we live in a self-correcting universe, where errors are corrected, where redemption is always available. It is quite possible and it would be highly beneficial not only to the family but to society as a whole, we believe, for a man and a woman to fall in love, and by strict mental discipline observe a monogamous and faithful sexual relationship. With chastity of mind and thought, most adults can forge a new path where they "foresake all others" in mind and memory and become as one, each ready to see the other reflected in their children.

9

CONCEIVE IN WEDLOCK

Figure 10. A pregnant women without a husband in her support system is exceedingly anxious and that anxiety depresses her unborn.

BOTH THE MOTHER AND THE FATHER of a child are aware that a new human requires enormous caretaking. Therefore, much guilt arises in both parents if that child does not have a guaranteed stable home in which to develop.

Even nature usually cooperates to ensure that the child will have "two hearts" to love him and at least four "eyes to watch over" him. In most cases, a teen-age girl will not conceive on her first "yielding to temptation."

Society often must bear part of the blame for teen-age promiscuity and pregnancy. The mating urge is very powerful in healthy young men and women. At times, it is the most powerful of all urges, as evidenced by the fact that young men and women will often risk their very lives in order to mate. More than that, television, films, novels, suggestive jokes, exaggerated ribald tales of older peers, and dozens of other forces and circumstances conspire to urge teen-agers to engage in the procreative sex act, and to do so very prematurely.

But, most societies do not adequately prepare their youth for the responsibilities of parenthood or adulthood. Most are structured so that youth cannot become economically independent until well into their twenties.

The typical university education, for example, does not even begin until the person is 18 years or so, and does not end until the person is well over 20. Is the person supposed to repress his or her sexual urges for eight to ten years? Obviously, this is an impossible expectation for most healthy people.

What is the solution?

In the future, it is our opinion, all societies will prepare their young people to be able to assume the responsibilities of adulthood, including parenthood, at a more realistic age. Under a better organized educational system that implements a more sensitive and realistic curriculum, both the mother and the father will have learned a "marketable skill" and should have had clinical training on how to fulfill the responsibilities of parenthood by the age of twenty.

In the meantime, a few far-sighted parents are encouraging their offspring to marry young, to continue their education during the early married years, alternating study semesters if necessary, and to begin their families while young.

Other equally healthy and normal young people control their reproductive drives by wholesome physical and intellectual activities which serve as sublimations or temporary substitutes for sexual activities. Catholicism and Buddhism, for example, have demonstrated that, for a time, all healthy men and women are perfectly capable of sublimating the sexual drive, for their own good and for the good of society as a whole. The temporary sublimation or sacrifice of sexuality is not, ultimately, a sacrifice at all. It is a down payment on a longer-term, more satisfying goal.

In whatever manner societies and concerned parents adjust to the conflicting urges and drives of the individual and the longer-term needs of human evolution, there is overwhelming and compelling evidence that the healthiest children, very measurably so, are those born to a young, economically secure, married couple and where the couple personally dedicate themselves to the rearing of those children.[26]

Concerned about the growing trend of young people in America to conceive babies out of wedlock, and aware of the enormous negative consequences of that alarming trend, one of the world's most famous and prestigious "think tanks," the Brookings Institution in Washington, D.C., conducted a thorough study of the feasibility of a national "Family Policy" for the United States. Drawing upon the best research and forward-look-ing ideas available, and attempting to urge America to move forward in strengthening the family, it wrote:

> In the ideal world, all families would be legally sanctioned units (i.e., marriages) of mature, self-supporting parents devoted to each other and to planned and healthy children whose activities would be supervised by the parents in a manner that optimized growth and development.[27]

In the absence of a national policy, religious and ethnic communities can promulgate this idea via their own educational programs. And stable families can begin educating their children to adhere to this idea.

In future we will educate intending parents to bring into being children that have a reasonable guarantee of living within a union secured by the sanctions of society and by love, a stable marriage.

---

26. The average age of Anne Roe's 64 scientists' mothers was just over 20, for example. As a woman ages so does her ova. And with age comes danger of damage to the ova. Thus as a woman ages her chances of giving birth to a child with a birth defect goes up. There are other advantages of having children early. If a woman reaches 40 and her children are now independent of her, she is now free to devote her mature intellect to benefit society in the workplace or in some civic or voluntary endeavor.

27. A Report, July, 1977.

10

LOVE THE OTHER PARENT

Figure 11. The child will reach age six before he sees his parents as one, as a team. Before that, the child oscillates his love between the parents. If the parents love each other, the child's psyche unites faster.

THE CHILD is, genetically, one half from one parent and one half from the other. This means, as is well-known, that the child's features, shape of head, nose, lips, eyes, ears, teeth, color of skin, hair, propensity for certain diseases etc., will resemble one or the other parent or, sometimes, as with complexion, be a compromise between the two. The infant's emotional styles (grumpy in the morning, cheerful in the evening, or the like), the postures assumed under certain conditions, mannerisms, facial expressions, speech patterns, and hundreds of discrete behavior patterns – many of which are silent or subliminal – will reflect both parents, just as physical attributes will reflect both.

When one parent sees the reflection of the other in the child's physical or emotional characteristics or in the child's overt or silent behavior, that parent reacts to those characteristics somewhat as he or she would react to the other parent. Not even the best professional actors in the world can disguise their true feelings 24 hours a day. In other words, if the mother loves the father, the mother will love nearly 100% of the child's characteristics and behavior patterns, which observably number in the thousands, even at the relatively primitive state of contemporary psychology.

Conversely, when antipathy exists between the parents, each parent may experience negative feelings toward those qualities in the child that remind that parent of the other.

Where the child's parents love each other and consequently love most of the reflections of each other in the child, and, perhaps more importantly, are tolerant of each other's shortcomings, the child has the best insurance policy against mental confusion and dysfunctional behavior. Moreover, the child in such a loving family will be free of the most common forms of stress in modern society – the threat of, or the actual break-up of the family.

Several studies have shown that stress reduces the mental functioning of a child. One study reported in the *New York Times*, May 31, 1983, controlled for every variable (age, sex, ethnic group, socio-economic status, religion, etc.) except stress in 4,000 children. The findings suggested that a stressful home "costs" the child an average of 12 intelligence points and, to a child, and what is more stressful than hostility between the parents?

When the parents love each other, the child's intelligence is not inhibited by the natural fears of losing one or both parents. In the security of a loving home, the child's higher, "supra-survival" powers, its exploratory urges, are free to experiment with the universe, to play, to enjoy meaningful conversation, to bask in a universe of love.[28]

---

28. In *The Making of a Scientist* Anne Roe paints a very instructive picture of the homes in which America's top 64 scientists grew up. The home was orderly, the father was successful in his profession, but he was not a "workaholic." He enjoyed coming home on time to be with his family for dinner, for example. The mother was very unstressed. She had an intelligence score about 13 points higher than that of her husband, loved to read, and read to her children a great deal. There was religion in the home. The lesson from Roe was that the parents were truly mated. They loved each other. (The book includes two marginal exceptions, two divorces. But those divorces did not occur until the child had passed middle childhood, at ages 11 and 13).

11

STRENGTHEN THE MOTHER'S BODY

AS PLATO SAID MORE than two thousand years ago, a healthy mind requires a healthy body.

Obviously, the new human has to draw nourishment for its body from the body of its mother. If the mother's body is strong and functioning well then the child's chances of obtaining the right nutrients, hormones, and enzymes at exactly the right times will be high. If, on the other hand, the mother's body is functioning poorly – through malnutrition, disease, or stress – it can hardly be expected to serve the second body's crucial first nine months.

The mother should, therefore, have a complete physical examination before allowing herself to become pregnant. She should correct all possible deficiencies such as being overweight or underweight; having low red-blood cell count, etc.

Figure 12. Strenuous exercises stimulate the brain to produce endorphins which help induce a sense of physical and mental well-being.

(Even in areas where there are no "Western"-educated physicians, this physical examination is still possible. Most tribes or villages in the world will have sensitive "traditional" healers or senior men and women who are familiar with folk medicine. These men and women often are quite skillful in recommending the right herbs and natural foods for pregnant women. For example, in certain areas of Korea, by tradition, pregnant and nursing women will be encouraged to increase their intake of various kinds of seaweed, including *keem* (musubi nori), a rich source of vitamins and minerals, especially the metals needed by the developing brain, – iodine, zinc, iron, copper, etc.)

Having decided to become pregnant – and we do emphasize that this decision should be a conscious one for reasons to be discussed later – the future mother should then choose a physical regimen, a daily program of 15 to 30 minutes of strenuous exercises, that brings her body up to or near the standard of an athlete. That is, her muscle tone and control should be functioning near maximum efficiency. In this way, her body can serve two bodies and the complex and highly strenuous natural birthing process will be much less painful and damaging to both individuals.[29]

There are several good exercise books with special body-strengthening programs for pregnant women. We recommend that the future mother examine several of these and choose one or more as her guide during this the most critical period in the life of her child.[30]

We emphasize the physical because at this early stage in the child's development, it is almost impossible to separate the functions of the mind from the functions of the body. For example, during the nine prenatal months the infant's brain will grow 100,000,000,000 brain cells, or neurons. Each neuron must grow to exceed in complexity and strength the most powerful computer chip known. Each neuron must grow a sheath or an insulation around itself, and some neurons must form up to 10,000 chemical and electrical connections with other neurons. At certain growth stages this can amount to producing more than 4,000 new neurons per second and more than 40,000,000 new connections per second! Such incredibly

---

29. The pioneering French gynecologist and obstetrician, Frédérick Leboyer, reminded both mothers and fathers of the importance of the mother being physically fit so as to increase the chances of a healthy childbirth. Dr. Leboyer oversaw the births of thousands of babies during his career and in 1953 was promoted to the post of Chef de Clinique of the University of Paris Faculty of Medicine.

30. While we urge the mother to stay fit during pregnancy, J. Brody, writing in the *New York Times*, February 2, 1994, "Fitness and the Fetus: A turnabout in advice," (p. C13), cautions that fitness can be overdone by pregnant women.

rapid multiplication of cells and such prodigious "circuit building" by the brain require that the chemical balances in the brain be maintained at optimal levels. The maintaining of an optimal state of health so that the baby's brain can efficiently build itself requires that the mother's body be chemically and electrically[31] in perfect physical condition.

Obviously, each brain cell is an "individual" with its own nutritional needs, its own timing schedule, and its own functions to perform. For example, the brain cells that control the development of the infant's leg muscles must become "adult" early in the prenatal stage of the infant's development. Each function represents an aspect of intelligence: stimulus reception, memory, stimulus transmission, etc. For example, every time the infant kicks, a lengthy and pleasurable "electrical" circuit is knitted in the brain, never to be completely forgotten or lost and always to be available to the person to train itself to perform even more complex bodily motions.

We know that the intelligence of a person is never fixed. But if the mother's body does not provide the right nourishment and the right chemical balances so that the infant's brain can develop properly, the child's mental functioning will certainly have very low upper limits. Those limits will not have been set by genetic factors, but the physical and emotional climate within the womb.

The mother's first task, after becoming pregnant, is to remove every possible obstacle from the infant's goal of building his own unique copy of Plato's perfect and ideal brain. The infant can do that only if the mother's body is as near perfect as possible. This task *is* within the mother's control.

---

31. Neurons greatly resemble electrical wires. Thus, by "electrically" we mean that each neuron must be sheathed or insulated in order not to short-circuit. This perfect sheathing will happen only if the mother's body is functioning optimally.

Part III
Some Specific Suggestions
After Conception

12

THE MOTHER TAKES NO DRUGS

HEALTHY MOTHERS NEED no drugs. Unhealthy women should not allow themselves to become pregnant: the risks for the infant are too great.

Even aspirin, a relatively harmless drug, has negative effects upon the fetus.[32] The smoking mother's infant at birth weighs one to two pounds less than normal.[33] The infant of the alcohol-drinking mother often shows a lower intelligence score than children born from normal mothers. The general rule, undisputed by any authority that we know of, is that the mother takes no drugs during pregnancy. Vitamins, minerals and other dietary supplements such as seaweed extract and the like, are not, of course, considered drugs.

At one time in Western medicine there was the notion that relatively mild chemicals did not cross the "placental barrier." We now know that such notions were naive and, frequently, dangerous to the infant. (Most traditional medical practices that we know of did not take such a naive view,

---

32. "Studies in humans have not shown that aspirin causes birth defects. However, studies in animals have shown that aspirin causes birth defects." See the Mayo Clinic Health Letter, July 05, 1995. (www.mayoclinic.com). We caution the reader that, typically, "birth defects" are reported only for gross deformities. Damage to the brain, typically, are not reported as a "birth defect."

33. The Voice of America in its April 1, 1979, "Science Report," carried around the world, featured a study that showed that cigarette smoking damaged the placenta of women even *before* the placenta was formed. This and even more alarming drug-abuse findings help to explain the world-wide epidemic of brain-damaged babies. The significance of this report is very great, because in some biological and chemical aspects—though not morphological aspects—the embryo and the placenta are twins.

preferring the view that the infant is highly sensitive to everything in its environment, even – or perhaps especially – during the first few weeks of life). Even the chemicals produced in the mother's body cross the placenta and affect the fetus. When the mother is angry or in a state of extreme fright, the fetus displays some of the same physical movements, expressions, and chemical changes as the mother. And, conversely, when the mother is happy or enraptured, say by music, the infant's body speaks a language of happiness or rapture too.[34]

Many tribes of the world go much farther than Western society and adhere to all sorts of taboos about what the mother may or may not do, so as to give the unborn a "fair" chance in the world – or at least they used to. The mother may not go to a funeral lest the grief cause the child to be morose; she may not be frightened lest the child be cowardly. And we know of no traditional society that tolerated intoxication in the pregnant mother.

Pregnant women should also be aware that the natural body is often a better pharmacological factory than the best pharmaceutical house: when the woman is healthy and sensitive and not under stress, the brain, when necessary, will

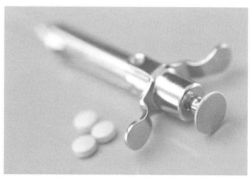

Figure 13. The human brain is still a mystery. Each cell or neuron, according to the science and science-fiction writer Isaac Asimov, can control up to 10,000 leg muscles, for example. Each cell learns, remembers and, in some senses, thinks. Nearly all drugs damage some brain cells or neurons. Narcotics damage nearly all important brain cells.

---

34. "The elements of music, namely tonal pitch, timbre, intensity and rhythm, are also elements used in speaking a language. For this reason, (prenatal) music prepares the ear, body and brain to listen to, integrate and produce language sounds. Music can thus be considered a pre-linguistic language which is nourishing and stimulating to the whole human being, affecting body, emotions, intellect, and developing an internal sense of beauty, sustaining and awakening the qualities in us that are wordless and otherwise inexpressible" See Giselle E. Whitwell, "The Importance of Prenatal Sound and Music" (Undated) Whitewell also points out that one reason that the quality of our spoken languages has recently diminished is that mothers no longer sing lullabies to their prenates as much as they once did.

direct the production of the safest pain-killers known. One of these, similar in fact to opium, is produced by the mother just before delivery.

The point is that under *most* conditions, all foreign drugs are dangerous to the child and are unnecessary for the mother.[35]

---

35. Thalidomide was an often-prescribed tranquilizer for pregnant women, particularly in Britain, Germany and in the U.S. Frequently, the babies of such mothers were born without limbs or parts of their limbs. We know of no drug that is without side effects. In addition to avoiding all drugs, the pregnant woman should significantly increase her intake of water (at least 12 glasses per day). Her kidneys are now processing the waste materials of two bodies and her sweat glands are working overtime, too. (Research has shown that when adults increase their intake of water to 10 glasses per day, they reduce their infectious disease rate by 65%).

13

THE FATHER TO KEEP THE MOTHER'S MIND PEACEFUL

ROBERT A. LEVINE, a professor of anthropology, then at Chicago, now at Harvard, was so impressed by the mental precocity manifested by some tribal East African infants shortly after birth that he obtained a large research grant from the Carnegie Foundation to find out the mechanisms for such a striking fact. In one publication, Dr. LeVine suggested that one reason for the precocity of African infants was the ambience of affection that surrounded the mother during her pregnancy.[36, 37]

---

36. See Robert A. LeVine, "Africa" in F. L. K. Hsu (Ed.), *Psychological Anthropology*. Homewood, Illinois: Dorsey Press, 1961. See also M. Geber, "The Psychomotor Development of African Children in the First Year and the Influence of Maternal Behavior," *Journal of Social Psychology*, 1958, 47, 185-195; and J. L. Evans, *Children in Africa: A Review of Psychological Research*. New York: Columbia University, Teachers College, 1970.

LeVine also writes, "Using Gesell tests for infants past the neonate stage and methods devised by Andre Thomas for testing neonates, (Marcelle) Geber found striking evidence of precocity in African infants. Nine-hour-old infants drawn into a sitting position were able to prevent their heads from falling back, which European children cannot do until six weeks after birth. (Marcelle) Geber suggests that the initial precocity might be due to the attitude of the pregnant mother. The arrival of the baby is always looked forward to with great pleasure . . . and is not a source of anxiety." (p. 24)

37. Matt Ridley (2003) in his excellent summary of the influence of "nurture" on "nature," or the reciprocal effect of environment on genes found reason to give substantial negative weight to the influence of stress on human behavior and on the physical and emotional health of the individual. The father's role in keeping the mother's mind peaceful is not sufficiently stressed in any of the more than 50 cultures that we have lived in or visited.

In her state of being carefully protected and indulged, the newly pregnant mother experiences a glowing feeling of well-being. That mental sense of worth affects her muscles, which also relax. This muscular relaxation allows or encourages the fetus to move around more in the womb. And, it is believed, every single movement of the fetus coincides with the construction of neural networks and facilitates the development of communication channels within the brain – at the most appropriate time.[38]

And when the mother is in a state of well-being, not only are her muscles affected, her hormonal secretions are affected as well. Apparently, adrenalin, even in minute quantities, is a poison to the fetus, except just before birth. The absence of adrenalin allows the endorphins and other natural "pleasure chemicals" to stimulate the brain and produce a state of mind close to serenity or even ecstasy. Leboyer in his classic, *Birth Without Violence*, offers several photographic evidences for this inference.

The chain of "causation" for such a remarkably high advantage in the tribal neonate seems to us perfectly logical. Reasoning backwards: the tribal African newborn is more intelligent; it is more intelligent because the uterus was relaxed and not poisoned by adrenalin; the uterus was not poisoned and was relaxed because the mother was protected as much as possible from every stress and was encouraged to maintain her emotions in a state of well-being; she could maintain that state of well-being because the husband/father was assigned, by tradition, the duty to make her feel so; and the husband/father, in turn was assisted and supported by the entire village structure and life-style. The culture reflected a social policy that the society must be supportive of the father and the mother and the baby.[39]

---

38. On average, 4,000 neurons, or brain cells, must be created in the fetus' brain every second; 240,000 every minute, and many of those neurons will establish up to 10,000 connections with other neurons. With some of those connections being concerned with muscular coordination, and being established early in the womb-life, the village child had, indeed, a head start over infants raised in a less benevolent environment. What a strange universe it would be if such prodigious and wonderful efforts by the growing brain were not related to the emotional and physiological state of the mother. Ancient African belief systems agreed with Western philosophy: everything in the environment influences everything else.

Figure 14. Pregnancies soften the hearts of mothers – and of fathers. Pregnancy is also a time of great stress for a mother, who knows that many dangers lurk around her. A loving husband's close presence assuages much of that anxiety. Professor Burton White, once at Harvard, recommends that in the future both parents will not work during the period of the pregnancy. They will spend much time together studying the biology, the sociology, and the psychology of what is happening to all three individuals.

Another way to give the neonate an early developmental advantage was discovered by some experimenting South Africans who adapted an iron lung by reversing it to produce a partial vacuum from the pregnant woman's midriff downward. In that reversed and artificial partial vacuum chamber, the pregnant women could relax for about two hours a day. The device operated very simply. It helped to relax the abdominal muscles of the mother, producing some of the same physical and psychological effects as a benevolent village life. The results: the babies born where the mothers used the modified iron lung had intelligence scores 10 or 15 points (10 to 15 percent) higher than what would have been statistically predicted or expected.

What can the father do to discharge his responsibility to protect the developing brain of his child?

We urge every expecting father to use his ingenuity to find ways to reduce his wife's anxieties to the lowest possible level so that their child will have the advantages that a low-stress pregnancy gives to both mother and child. These advantages include, of course, a more perfectly wired brain, which translates into a more efficient brain. This advantage is immediately measurable by such tests as the Gesell tests and the

---

39. This idyllic picture, alas, is much less true today than almost 50 years ago when the comparative advantage of tribal village life on the intelligence of the child was discovered by Marcel Geber and others. Also, unfortunately, even then, the advantages enjoyed by the village baby at birth were soon lost – usually by 24 months, according to LeVine. This loss reflected the failure of the mother, the father, and the village to do some of the other things recommended in this book, or recommended by sound national family and educational policies.

Apgar test, which is now standard in the United States immediately following birth.

Here are some examples of how the father may assist his wife to obtain two extra hours of rest per day:

— If there is an overriding reason why the wife/mother must continue to work during her pregnancy, let the father consult with her and, if necessary, with her employer to negotiate a two-hour reduction in her work day.

— The father assumes some additional household chores so that the mother's duties in the home are significantly reduced.

— Reduce the family's social life.

— If there are older siblings, let the father organize them so that they take on a significant part of the task of keeping the household functioning efficiently.

Most societies have created many informal systems to facilitate the extra-rest requirement of the pregnant mother: in Fiji, often the wife's mother or younger sister or cousin moves in to help with the chores, or a neighboring friend does the laundry for the pregnant mother's older children. In Hausa land in Nigeria, by tradition, the father's parents take care of the older siblings in the household, thus greatly reducing the mother's chores and concerns.

Whatever the social mechanisms adopted, it is imperative that the newly pregnant mother be assisted in her homemaker duties and obtain at least 10 hours of sleep and rest every day. This time taken is an investment in the mental development of her unborn child, an investment that probably pays the highest dividends of any investment in the world!

14

THE MOTHER TO OBTAIN A COMPLETE MEDICAL EXAMINATION

THE MOMENT THE MOTHER discovers that she is pregnant she should make an appointment to see a very good and up-to-date physician. A good physician will insist upon a complete medical examination, for good reasons. For example, if the mother's red-blood cell count is low (which is the case in more than 50% of the mothers in the poorer parts of the world), this critical deficiency can normally be quickly corrected. It must be corrected because among other functions, the red-blood cells carry oxygen to the brain of both mother and child. The human brain, although but one to two percent of the body's weight, consumes more than 20 percent of the body's oxygen – oxygen which is carried only by red-blood cells. This enormously disproportionate consumption of oxygen by the brain suggests how important the mother's red-blood count is. She must not take chances with her child's brain.[40]

The good physician will check for other common causes of cellular distress in the fetus, such as diseases of various kinds. If, for example, either the father or the mother had

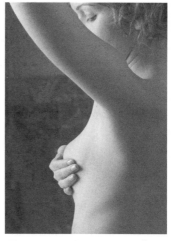

Figure 15. A woman performing a breast self-examination. Gradually, mankind is developing new methods for individuals to assess their own medical condition. Women now regularly check their breasts for lumps. Medical-testing kits to test for blood sugar and other indicators of health are becoming widespread. Pregnancy is a special time where expert examinations are especially necessary.

premarital sexual relations, it is crucial that the physician check for the presence of certain sexually transmitted diseases that may show no outward symptoms in the parents, but which, if present in the mother and uncorrected, may damage the infant's brain or other organs. Unfortunately, here is where traditional medicine, insofar as we know, lags behind Western medicine in coping with this relatively modern and widespread problem.

In many countries, and in rural areas of nearly all countries, the mother may be unable to find or to afford a physician to advise her at this critical time. For example, in some countries physicians are very scarce and concentrated in the larger cities (Iraq, 1 per 5,000 persons; Malawi, 1 per 76,000; Thailand, 1 per 7,600).[41] In case physicians are scarce or unaffordable, the mother can take matters into her own hands. She can increase her intake of mineral-rich and vitamin-rich foods. And she can consult traditional healers and midwives.

Most traditional healers and midwives will know which foods have been recommended for pregnant mothers from time immemorial. In Korea, for example, certain seaweeds are recommended to pregnant and nursing women. In parts of Africa, guava is recommended not only for its high vitamin-C content, but for its mineral content, as well. In the Pacific, certain fish are recommended, depending upon the area and season, along with certain iron-rich green leaves, roots, and berries.

We urge every pregnant mother to consult the wise elderly women and midwives in her society to learn a great deal of nutritional and folk-medicine information that is on the verge of extinction in most societies.

After the medical examination comes a planned regime of health maintenance. The basic elements of health maintenance are: food/nutrition; exercise; rest; avoidance of infection; avoidance of stress; and avoidance of extreme physical or emotional states. We emphasize that all of those factors ought to be *controlled*, consciously controlled, in so far as possible by the mother, with the help of her husband.

---

40. Like many writers, Matt Ridley (1999 and 2003) offers abundant reasons for this advice. The formation of the complex network of neurons in the brain is such a monumental "manufacturing" task that the least imbalance of chemicals or hormones can have harmful consequences.

41. Source: *Encyclopaedia Britannica*, "Public Health Services".

With respect to exercise, nearly all of the "Natural Childbirth" methods that we know of train the mother in some regime to strengthen her abdominal muscles. The mother is advised to consult, if possible, and, if so inclined, to follow one of these methods. Most libraries and full-service bookstores will be able to provide the books describing the "Natural Childbirth" methods. These are the methods of Dr. Ferdinand Lamaze of France who developed his method from a system devised in the 1920s in the Soviet Union[42]; the method of Dr. Robert Bradley in Colorado in the U.S.; and the method of Dr. Grantley Dick-Read of Britain.

All of these modern "natural" methods, plus some other approaches, including some traditional midwifery methods as practiced in most parts of the world, have as a primary goal the strengthening of the mother's body so that she may participate actively in the birthing process. The organ and function that most such natural methods focus upon are the diaphragm, the midriff muscles, and breathing. When these muscles and this function are strong, the child being born has something strong to push against and receives greater help from its mother. When the mother's body is strong, Lamaze and Leboyer report, the fetus does not go into high anxiety, it feels the mother's competent help. It enjoys a beautiful birth.[43]

The purposes of the medical examination are manifold: to rule out all diseases; to confirm a health-maintenance and exercise plan for the mother; and to give to the mother the confidence that she can handle the coming "blessed event," that she is going to make that event a blessing for her family that will, in no wise, be an event of stress or unnecessary anxiety.

Only the healthy mother can be "in charge" of her body.

---

42. See www.lamaze.org
43. For a full treatment of this topic see Leboyer, *Birth Without Violence*.

15

INSPIRE THE MOTHER

MOST BOOKS FOR the expectant mother hardly discuss the prenatal period of the infant. One reason for this systemic oversight is that very little research has been done on external influences on the prenatal infant, a situation that we urge intelligent mothers and fathers to help correct. We think that this is one of the richest areas for significant research over the next few years.

We suspect that the old wives' tales of mothers suddenly becoming interested in inspirational music or art during pregnancy just might have more than a grain of truth in them.

Is it not logical that the emotional state of the mother would somehow influence the emotional condition – and possibly, the experiments suggest, emotional inclinations – of her prenatal child? Indeed, some experiments have been conducted with pregnant animals that suggest the contagion of emotions across the placenta. If the host mother manifests fear, the fetus manifests the muscle behavior associated with fear, making the body smaller, tightening the abdominal muscles, etc. The inference is strong: a mother's emotions are, in fact, transmitted in some form to the infant.

Certainly, the infant in the womb responds to different rhythms differently and seems to prefer certain rhythms (baroque, for example) over others (rock and roll).

Would it do any harm to either the infant or to the mother if she were to enjoy a good concert of music by Mozart or enjoy a visit to a museum or art gallery to see a show of Bernard Leach or of Mark Tobey or of Raphael?

We think it would do the mother good. Great art elevates the senses and sensibilities, knocks on the door of the higher consciousness and attempts to educate the higher powers of the mind about nature and man and tries to refine the senses' appreciation for that which is "good and true and beautiful," the central foci of philosophy.

Great art and great music inspire the mother, obviously, cause her to elevate her thoughts, soothe her fears and cause her, a primary vehicle of life, to love life with all its glorious potentials – and occasional dangers. Great art and great music give her a hint or a glimpse of heaven, the goal that she consciously or unconsciously cherishes for her child.

Other ways of inspiring the mother include:

— Taking her for a leisurely stroll in a lovely garden or park where she may study the beautiful trees, flowers, shrubs, and wildlife.

— Complimenting her on some simple act of kindness that she did.

— Reading to her or giving her a biography of some great and influential person.[44]

— Taking her to see a movie that is aesthetically and morally pleasing. Such a movie would give us a vivid picture of history, heightens our admiration for superb acting – another inspiring art form – and, for a short period of time, helps us to discharge our anxieties and worries and helps us to get lost in timelessness. Surely, this too is a healthy experience.

— The father can begin to educate any older children about the necessity to protect the mother from any undue stress, and help them to become active participants in this major family event.

Obviously, in this lesson we have only touched the surface of this "game of life."

One often hears women ask children, "Why are you so pretty?" (or "handsome?") Clearly, the child would not know the answer to such a blushing question. But there are answers, some observational and some based upon genetic research. Our combined experiences of over forty years in many

---

44. Among those recommended are: Abraham Lincoln, Mahatma Gandhi, George Washington Carver, Marie Curie, Maria Montessori, Albert Einstein, Constantine, Emperor Meiji, Arthur Rubinstein, or almost any one of the Nobel Laureates.

different cultures suggest that pretty and handsome children most often come from mothers who were frequently inspired during their pregnancy.[45]

---

45. Matt Ridley's review of the research (1999) of how genetics operate in the physiological formation of the individual confirms this sociological observation. Mothers under less stress produce babies who have greater bodily symmetry. According to classical Greek thought, symmetry is, typically, the dominant aspect of beauty. Ridley found that children's whose faces were highly asymmetrical endured greater intrauterine stress.

Ridley writes, "In early 1990s there was revived an old interest in bodily symmetry, because of what it can reveal about the body's development during early life. Some asymmetries in the body are consistent: the heart is on the left side of the chest, for example, in most people. But other smaller asymmetries can go randomly in either direction. In some people the left ear is larger than the right; in others, vice versa. The magnitude of this so-called fluctuating asymmetry is a sensitive measure of how much stress the body was under when developing, stress from infections, toxins or poor nutrition. The fact that people with high IQs have more symmetrical bodies suggest that they were subject to fewer developmental stresses in the womb or in childhood. Or, rather, that they were resistant to such stresses." (p.89)

16

PRAY FOR THE EMBRYO

STUDIES OF THE FORCES operating on the prenatal child are beginning to take on the respectability of scientific rigor. And we should soon begin to see some revolutionary ideas of how the infant in the womb is affected by external forces – forces of all types.

Until recently, science did not encourage interdisciplinary research or holistic research. Science was "disciplined," that is, each branch of science pursued its own questions. And since there was no over-arching science concerned with the prenatal child, there was little research concerning this life-stage.

One of the factors spurring more scientific study of what is happening to the child in the uterus or womb was the documentation that thalidomide, a strong tranquilizer, has very serious negative effects on the physical development of the fetus. Children whose mothers took thalidomide frequently were born without one or more of their limbs.

Other more voluntary and positive studies have shown that the fetus responds to musical rhythms and to the moods of the mother and sometimes mirrors her bodily reactions.

In another realm of research, small bits of evidence are beginning to show that prayer has more than gross physiological effects. We have known for decades that prayer relaxes, or sets in motion a chain of events that results in relaxation; that prayer changes the wave pattern of the brain and measurably reduces the production of certain chemicals which, when in excess supply, serve as the body's own internal poisons. Adrenalin is one.

If prayer has such gross physiological effects, might it not have subtle neurological effects? Two distinguished researchers, Andrew Newberg, M.D.

and Eugene D'Aquili, M.D., Ph.D. found compelling evidence that prayer does have several physiological consequences. They found the specific location in the brain where religious experiences such as prayer are manifested. (*Why God Won't Go Away*, 2001.)

Many people intuitively or by tradition, believe as we do, that prayer also has spiritual effects. Man is still a mysterious being. We all assume that man has a mind, but no one has seen a mind. It would appear obvious, then, that if the mind is mysterious, part of its mystery lies in the fact that it is not a material thing. It cannot obey the laws of physical things, since it is not a physical thing. (This would be like air obeying all the laws of water.) The mind must therefore obey other laws. Could some of those other laws be hidden in mankind's large library of prayers?[46]

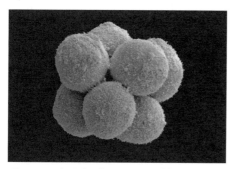

Figure 16. The long view of history confirms the power of prayer. Societies that believe in prayer outlive societies that do not. Babies sense the climate of prayer that surrounds them and they thereby develop a loyalty to their society. Image: scanning electron micrograph of a human embryo at day 3.

Perhaps it would be helpful, at this point, to clarify one aspect of prayer. We imagine that man attempts to misuse prayer as he misuses dynamite or fire. We suggest that perhaps the laws of the universe do not allow the answering of inappropriate prayers. This fact may have helped to lead to the extinction of praying behavior in a large mass of humanity, who could not discern when to pray for something and when not to.

We imagine that prayer must always be a positive force, not a force that aims to suspend the laws of the universe. (Is it not absurd to leap from a tall building and then to ask in prayer to be saved from gravity?)

---

46. By "prayer" we don't mean only a ritualistic or dogmatic prayer. Prayer may have many forms. And, in a sense, positive thoughts may be seen as having the effect of a prayer, "I ask the universe to bestow its blessings upon this child." Prayer may be defined as a conversation with the Consciousness of the universe. It may also be defined as a dialog with nature, as communing with the unconscious mind, etc.

We imagine, instead, that prayer is a force to magnify the positive forces operating in our universe. There is substantial evidence that healing after a heart attack takes place much faster in a prayerful environment than in an indifferent one.

But the greatest evidence for the power of prayer lies in macro history: no society has achieved long-term stability and a high level of culture without a powerful and nearly universal habit of regular prayer. Indeed, one of the greatest heroes of Western Civilization, the Emperor Constantine, was born to a mother, Helen, who lived almost constantly in a state of prayer. The historian Edward Gibbon regarded Constantine as one of the truly noble men of history and, by his famous narrative, *The Decline and Fall of the Roman Empire*, let us believe that there might have been a cause-and-effect relationship. George Bernard Shaw extolled the saintly nature of Joan of Arc, confirming her habits of regular prayer. Thomas Carlyle, the great British historian, offered other models of this idea, Frederick the Great of Germany, for example.

But the absence of evidence may be more compelling: we can not recall one great idea that moved mankind forward that was born to a profane person.

Our universe cannot be just unless an equal chance is given to all humans from the moment of conception onward. Every child deserves, as a birthright, whatever advantage that prayer has to offer.[47]

---

47. Duncan Walker writes in the Newsletter of the National Institutes of Health (NIH), "People have used prayer and other spiritual practices for their own and others' health concerns for thousands of years. Scientific investigation of these practices has begun quite recently. . . to better understand whether they work. . . . The National Center for Complementary and Alternative Medicine (NCCAM) is supporting research in this arena. "Many Americans are using prayer and other spiritual practices. This was confirmed by findings from the largest and most comprehensive survey to date on Americans' use of complementary and alternative medicine. "Prayer was the therapy most commonly used among all the CAM therapies included in the survey. . .

"Catherine Stoney of NCCAM . . . noted: "There is already some preliminary evidence for a connection between prayer and related practices and health outcomes. For example, we've seen some evidence that . . . religious practices are associated with health and mortality – in other words, with better health and longer life. Such connections may involve immune function, cardiovascular function, and/or other physiological changes."

Part IV
Some Specific
Suggestions During Birth

17

USE A BIRTHING STOOL, SQUAT OR WATER BIRTH

SOME YEARS AGO while residing in Korea, one of the authors was shocked to learn that rural Korean women gave birth in the squatting position. "Don't they let them lie down and rest during birth?" he naively asked. His question betrayed several misconceptions.

First of all, the recently adopted prone position is not in harmony with the law of gravity. Thus, lying down is the wrong position from which to give birth. The only worse position for the mother is to stand on her head, or upside-down.

If one examines, even superficially, the anatomy of a woman, it becomes clear that the fetus should present itself not against the mother's curved backbone – which it would do if she were prone – but against the largest opening in the mother's body; her birth canal. This the child does if the mother is squatting or on a birthing stool. The mother must be in such a position that gravity can work *with* her and her baby. She should not be in a position where they are working against gravity.[48]

Figure 17. This image of a woman giving birth is from a 15th-century woodprint in a book by Eucharius Roeslin. Until the 18th century, nearly all cultures recommended birthing stools or squatting for the least painful and least dangerous delivery. One of the earliest written references to the birthing stool is at the time of Moses (Exodus 1:16).

The second error contained in the question implied an endorsement of the then current practice that someone other than the mother was "in charge" of the birthing process. The mother should be so acutely sensitive, in such near-perfect physical condition, so alertly aware of everything that is taking place in her body and in the body of her infant, that she should decide when she is to "rest". She must know when the next strong pang is coming and know when rest is appropriate. No one should "let" her do anything. She must be in charge, as was, in fact, the case with that unusually physically strong and robust race, the Koreans.

His third error was in speaking of "rest" at all. The time of birth is a period of both intense activity and relatively reduced activity, but not really rest as it is commonly understood. Therefore, the mother must relate to both extremes of her will, a test of self-control. It is a trial of all of her earlier preparation: physical and emotional. Giving birth is not a time for rest.

The "right" position for the body of the healthy mother – we are excluding cases where Cesarean sections are indicated – is the most open position she can assume. Many cultures, in addition to the Korean, entirely agree. It was only after Western medical practice began treating pregnancy and childbirth as "illnesses" that mothers assumed the prone position. They are not ill, at least most are not. In fact, during this period, their bodies are the most efficient they ever will be.

And to make delivery as comfortable as possible for the mother and facilitate her taking the most open position possible, several cultures have designed birthing stools for this exciting but extremely taxing event.

In most modern cultures the majority of people have never heard of birthing stools. We suggest that some clever entrepreneurs will serve both mankind and themselves by revising this ancient and kindly concern for both mother and baby.

One of the reasons for this suggestion is that most brain damage, after that caused by prenatal drugs and stress, can be attributed to damaging birthing procedures, for example, the improper use of forceps. In the San Joaquin Valley of California, a conference on special education in 1976

---

48. "Radiological evidence demonstrates a 28% increase in the overall area of the outlet with the squatting position compared with the supine position, resulting in obvious benefits to the progress and ease of birth." (Diane M. Fraser and Margaret Cooper (Eds.), *Myles Textbook for Midwives*. Edinburgh, U.K.: Churchill Livingston. 2003, p. 431

reported that 11% of the children in that relatively wealthy region were so severely damaged by the time they entered school that they required special teaching. The conference went on to assert that the real percentage of children so damaged as to need special education was closer to 25%.

Obviously, a large percentage of those damaged children were, in fact, injured by faulty birthing procedures.

The resurrection of the birthing stool, used in conjunction with water birthing, would go a long way toward preventing unnecessary injury to both mother and infant.[49]

The modern version of natural childbirth, which is relatively painless and much more protective of the newborn than previous methods, was pioneered by Russian obstetricians in the 1920s and carried forward by two French physicians, Ferdinand Lamaze and Frédérick Leboyer. (See Frédérick Leboyer, *Birth Without Violence*, 1975, and www.lamaze.org.) We believe that future birthing procedures will be more natural, much safer, much less painful to both mother and infant and more family oriented. The first Director of Harvard's Child Development Center, Dr. Burton White, and many other experts, also recommend that women time their child bearing to coincide with that period of their lives when giving birth is easier and less dangerous to them, in their late teens and early twenties. This recommendation obviously assumes some changes from the present pattern when women are giving birth much later in their lives than biology would seem to recommend.

---

49. France and New Zealand are leading a new birthing trend where the mother gives birth in a modified warm-water bath. The advantages to the mother for such a system are self-evident. Warm water relaxes, the buoyancy should help promote "rest" for various lower muscles of her body, and the birthing environment itself becomes the bathing environment with blood and other fluids disposed of in the circulating water.

18

NO DRUGS DURING BIRTHING

IT IS PAINFUL to give birth. Muscles and bones must stretch and contract, nerve paths must be disturbed, blood vessels must be squeezed, and blood supplies temporarily interrupted. Many bodily manufactured chemicals must also be properly shuttled to the right points, and many more functions must take place in the context we might liken to "crisis management." Often the pain and the distress is so great that the mother screams out in agony. (But in some cultures the mothers do not scream out. They have been trained or conditioned to control or to cope with those crises and pains).

There is often a temptation in such cases, especially in modern hospitals where painkillers are looked upon favorably, to allow the mother some pain-killing drug. This temptation to use them should be resisted as much as possible.

One of the virtues of the Lamaze natural childbirth method is that it obviates the need for painkillers through a strong regimen of strenuous exercises, both physical and mental, to prepare the mother for birth.

Strong pain-killers do more than kill pain. These drugs also deaden reflexes and disturb the body's own analgesic-producing mechanisms. With such strong, unnatural drugs, the mother and the child become passive "participants" in the birthing process, rather than active partners in charge of the process.

In the normal birth, the major actor is the infant. He moves his head at just the right time; he pushes his momentarily strong feet and legs against the mother's tight diaphragm; he folds or contracts his shoulders and twists his body through the birth canal with amazing skill and dexterity, almost as though some gold-medal-winning coach had drilled him in the little tricks of running the most difficult obstacle course in life.

But if he is drugged – and the infant is drugged whenever the mother is drugged – he cannot react with that acute sensitivity of the "Olympic-trained" athlete. He cannot control his muscles. There is a great gap between will and action. So, he warps his soft facial bones against his mother's tougher bones, which will make him less attractive. He moves his pliable skull bones against his mother's unmoving pelvic bones, which may disturb some brain tissue which, in turn, would reduce his future abilities to perceive, to process information, to remember. In short, his loss of control of his body during the birthing process results in a loss of brain function.[50]

And, being drugged, he will be more passive, less alert, insensitive to his mother's feelings. So, he tears and damages his mother's reproductive system, which, of course, helps neither him nor his future siblings.

Some mammals, who are some of man's closest anatomical cousins, apparently experience little or no pain in giving birth. But the price that mankind, or at least the women of mankind, must pay for the enormous brain that we have and that must be protected by a hard skull is the few hours of pain that the emergence of such a large head causes. Nature or evolution must have decided that the value of a large and potentially powerful

Figure 18. The Natural Childbirth movement pioneered by Dr. F. Lamaze and many others is now popular in several parts of the world, most notably in France and New Zealand. With proper pre-birth exercises, with a strong support team, particularly a dedicated husband, and a birthing tub, a woman, under normal conditions, does not need any artificial drug. Her brain supplies a chemical that is similar to opium for the most painful stages of the birth, and with no negative consequences. The baby in this photo was just delivered by water birth.

---

50. See Leboyer, Frédérick, *Birth Without Violence.*

brain was well worth the price. Would we, the human race, have it any other way?

Nature often is more clever than man. Nature produces sufficient and perfect pain-killers so as to optimize all factors: brain and skull size, birth canal size, and the mother's tolerance for pain. And, to be on the safe side, when the mother will have been carefully protected in her pregnancy, nature produces in the mother's brain the finest possible pain-killers, not enough to entirely eliminate pain, and not so much as to cause any chemical damage or mental retardation in the infant.

Nature's message is quite easy to read: she wants the baby born wide awake, ready to bond with an alert and caring mother.

19

MONITOR THE BIRTHING ROOM TEMPERATURE

THE IDEAL ROOM TEMPERATURE at delivery time should be near the same temperature as that of the womb, 98.6° Fahrenheit or 37° Centigrade.

Even toughened adults can experience discomfort when they move from a warm environment to a cold environment. A change of temperature as little as 10 degrees can be discomforting even to adults.

How can such a "minor" thing as a cold room have a negative effect upon a child? We as a species have largely grown out of the notion that the fetus and the new baby are unthinking, unfeeling. The fetus begins to "think" several weeks after conception, if not sooner – not complex thoughts that we call "thinking," but simple thoughts, simple but still on an elevated plane. A "thought" may be conceived as an electrical or chemical signal that goes from one neuron to another with the effect of producing movement or a change of perception. Every "thought" leaves a trace of itself. That is, it is remembered, it becomes a part of the history of that organism, part of its identity.

Long before birth, the brain-wave pattern of the fetus is almost indistinguishable from that of the sleeping infant. Every time an infant moves his foot or finger, he is thinking. More than that, he is building ever-increasing networks of complex communication channels to support future thinking. This building process begins a few weeks after conception.

Several weeks before birth the brain is active, forming impressions of a world it is soon to inherit. Will it be hostile or friendly? Imagine yourself visiting a foreign country and the first thing they do to you at the entry point is place you in a cold and unfamiliar environment. Would you have good feelings toward such a country? In the uterus, the fetus is naturally comfortable with its temperature. Therefore, for the infant, the ideal room temperature is near the temperature of the "country" he just left.

Figure 19. The baby lives in the womb at 98.6 degrees Fahrenheit or 37 degrees Centigrade. Any considerable temperature change at birth is uncomfortable for the infant. Most hospital delivery rooms are maintained at much colder temperatures relative to the womb environment.

An insensitive world is not one that a child wishes to explore intellectually. The explorer, whether of the physical or intellectual worlds, is one who sees the universe as essentially benevolent, or one in which he is not in peril. The explorer is one who is taught from birth, or before, that the universe is to be trusted, therefore to be understood, therefore to be explored. This idea and this attitude precede the development of the intellect. The individual's decision to develop his intellect is, in part, a response to his perception of the nature of the universe.

We recommend that attendants, and all those involved in the birth of the child, be sensitive to the need that the newborn not be shocked by large temperature differentials and other stimuli and ensure that the transition to a lower temperature after birth be gradual.[51]

---

51. Armed with a draft of this book, a famous sports attorney in Washington, D.C. who was pregnant asked her physician to keep the delivery room temperature close to the baby's body temperature. The physician immediately agreed. Our purpose here is to help mothers regain control over the entire birthing process. Mothers should seek the advice and assistance of obstetricians or midwives and other health care professionals, of course. Ultimately, mothers should be confident enough in their own knowledge and intuition to retain control over their bodies, especially in the critical moments surrounding the birth of their child. The fathers should support the mothers in this issue of control.

20

LIGHTS OUT, PLEASE

CATS SEE BETTER than people do. One reason is that nature seals kittens' eyelids until several days after birth.

Observant midwives, realizing that we humans can learn many things from nature, have made the same deduction, and protecting infants sensitive eyes from light is one of the duties of the midwife. Thus, all good midwives have a rule:

JUST BEFORE THE BABY'S HEAD IS PRESENTED, PLEASE TURN OUT OR DIM ALL LIGHTS.

Bright lights burn eye cells, just as sunlight burns skin cells.[52]

Hopefully, in the future, all babies will be born in rooms with soft lights, because it is not necessary for the mother or her attendants to see everything. Most humans are endowed with an acute sense of touch – which, of course, must be trained – and which should be used when the sense of sight is not appropriate. When the crown of the infant's head presents itself, the greatest crisis is over. In a few more seconds, another crisis will occur. But for a few seconds in the delivery room, indirect soft light, or no light at all, is the appropriate welcome for the newborn.

It is said that in ancient times, some humans could see the moons of Jupiter. First, they were not born in a time of extreme atmospheric pollution and, second, their midwives had the sensitivity and wisdom to dim the light of the room into which they were born, or to avoid using artificial bright light. Indeed, most midwives still follow the custom of darkening

---

52. See Leboyer, Frédérick, *Birth Without Violence*.

the room during the last moments of the birth. They have known intuitively or by tradition – for it was not established scientifically until recently – that bright light harms some of the cells of the eye.

Indeed, writer, Isaac Asimov wanted us to see the eye as a part of the brain, with each of the millions of eye cells more delicate than the finest computer chip that we routinely protect in the most sterile environment possible.

When we learn how to protect the infant's eyes, might our progeny, as our ancestors did, be able see the moons of Jupiter and other wonders of the universe? Certainly, they will see much better than our generation. And many of them will not need eyeglasses, since we will have learned to respect the integrity and sensitivity of those windows to the mind.

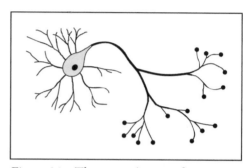

Figure 20. The neuron's axons function, in part, like electrical wires that must be carefully sheathed, lest they be subject to "short-circuiting." The sheathing really comes from the mother's nutritional care during pregnancy and the avoiding of harmful foods and drugs. At the end of one neuron's axons there may be as many as 10,000 synaptic buttons that carry the neuron's thoughts to other neurons, which diffuse those thoughts throughout the brain. Eye cells, much like brain cells, are very delicate, so much so that they can be destroyed by premature exposure to light.

As if to underscore the fact that at birth the eyes are not ready to be used, the newborn manifests high sensitivity to touch. Each sense has its own clock or time-table, so to speak. At birth, the sense that is "ripe" is the sense of touch. Sometimes, the sense of sight will ripen a few seconds later. Whenever it occurs, the "ripening" should not be hurried.

Lucky the infant whose mother and midwife respect his sensitive sense of touch and harmonize their senses with his.

Should not all children be so fortunate?

21

WAIT FOR THE UMBILICAL CORD TO COLLAPSE BEFORE CUTTING

ONE REASON THAT so many humans do not think alertly or efficiently is that at birth they lose too much of their blood.

The infant is so well designed that it normally does no bleeding in the birthing process, and for good reason. Blood is absolutely essential for the functioning of the entire body, especially the brain. Indeed, without oxygen for as little as 15 seconds, brain cells die. And brain cells are rarely replaced, unlike most other body cells and tissue.

Nature has mastered her task. As Joseph Chilton Pearce puts it, "barriers to intelligence have long since been winnowed out by nature because nature does not program for failure. Nature programs for success and has thus built a vast, an awesome program for success into our genes. What (nature) cannot program (against) is parental failure to nurture the infant child" (pp. 4-5).[53] And, we might add, nature cannot program against insensitivity and carelessness within humans.

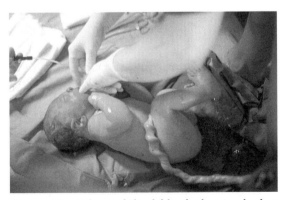

Figure 21. The umbilical blood, that is, the last blood from the mother's body, has been specially enriched by the mother's body for the first few moments of the infant's consciousness. In effect, those last few drops of blood are a powerful tonic.

After the baby emerges from the womb, several switches in the newborn's body must be turned from off to on and others from on to off. After several switches are activated, the umbilical cord collapses and the infant's powerful little heart will literally suck the last drop of blood from the umbilical cord into its body.

Only after the cord has collapsed and all the infant's blood is in his body should the umbilical cord be cut.

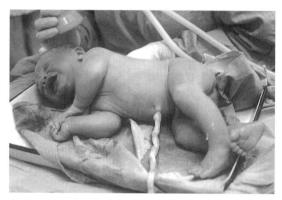

Figure 22. In too many instances, infants' umbilical blood is wasted. This can be avoided if the birth attendants follow the advice of Lamaze and Leboyer by cutting the umbilical cord after it has collapsed.

In the future, we believe, all children will be born in such loving, thoughtful societies that those involved in the birthing process will take care that there is no loss of the newborn's blood.

When there is a shortage of oxygen to the body, and all oxygen used by the body is carried by the blood, which part of the body will be most seriously affected?[54] Apparently, the body has its priorities right. The lower functions, heartbeat, breathing, etc., and the brain cells controlling those functions must be served first. When there is a shortage of blood (or oxygen), the functions that will be deprived first are the higher (more expendable) functions, the conscious and the self-conscious functions such as thinking and the control of feelings. We can reduce the incidence of brain damage by carefully protecting the infant's blood supply.

This is another reason for the mother to stay alert and "in charge" during the delivery. She will intuitively know that her baby's blood is precious, as is his intellect.

---

53. Pearce, Joseph Chilton, *Magical Child*. New York: E.P. Dutton. 1992, 1997.

54. The brain is the body's major user of blood and oxygen and the first part of the body to suffer if either is missing. A brain cell dies after 15 seconds if deprived of oxygen, never to live again.

The "perfect delivery" is rarely seen because it involves enormously complex variables including time, the mastery of which requires great patience.

Midwives usually learn through observation and experience that it sometimes takes the umbilical cord up to five minutes to collapse. Before it collapses, it performs its last function, if allowed enough time: it saturates the brain with an abundant supply of super-oxygenated blood.

Cutting the cord after it collapses and in a patient manner serves to diminish the shock of separation, also. When the cutting of the umbilical cord is mis-timed, several different kinds of damage may occur. The most serious threat posed by the premature cutting of the umbilical cord is that the infant's brain will be deprived of oxygen for a few seconds, or the supply will not be adequate. The baby's oxygen supply must come from its own lungs *before* the umbilical cord collapses and is cut. The oxygen supply must not be interrupted.[55]

The second threat is in the loss of the vehicles for oxygen, the red blood cells. Normally, the umbilical cord will collapse only after the infant's heart will have sucked into its body its own blood supply. But when the cord is snipped prematurely, there is the concomitant loss of vital blood.

A third danger is from infection via the umbilical cord. When the blood is still flowing into the infant's body from the umbilical cord, that flow naturally will carry with it every foreign organism that enters the blood stream, from the atmosphere in the room or from the knife used to cut the cord. But if the blood flow has ceased, the chances of germs flowing into the body is much less. (In some parts of the world one can identify which midwife performed which birth by studying the size of the children's navels. In some villages we have visited over half of the children will have enlarged navels, sometimes the size of a golf ball, indicating that the midwife did not use a sterile knife.)

The fourth danger is psychological, both to the baby and, to some degree, to the birth attendants, as well. When even the mildest forms of violence are practiced on the infant, we are conveying to that infant a powerful sig-

---

55. A study reported in the October 13, 2005, edition of the *New England Journal of Medicine* which followed 208 infants in 15 medical centers, found a connection between oxygen deprivation before, during or immediately after birth, and several severe disabilities, including blindness and cerebral palsy. (*The Arizona Republic*, October 16, 2005, p. A26.)

nal: "You have entered a violent world, baby. Survival here depends upon violence." Natural birth, in contrast, fosters the signals: "This is a kind world, baby. We behave here in conformity with nature's wisest ways."[56]

Might babies having the good fortune to be born under the eye of a midwife or physician who patiently wait for the umbilical cord to collapse before it is cut have, from that moment, an advantage over children having the misfortune to be delivered by an impatient birth attendant?[57] Might the differences be due, in part, to the fact that the brain is both a physiological organ with its own metabolic requirements, and because it is a sensitive, reactive, living thing, shriveling in the presence of violence and expanding in the presence of gentle, patient love?

The gentle touch, soft lights, normal body temperature, quietness, and patience with the umbilical cord all contribute to a perfect birth. Humanity now possesses nearly all of the physiological knowledge to make almost every birth "natural," relatively painless, and highly protective of the infant's delicate brain and emotional systems.

Natural childbirth fosters the signal: "THIS IS A KIND WORLD, BABY."

---

56. The advice to wait for the umbilical cord to collapse or stop pulsating before cutting, is consistent with many publications produced in recent years by the World Health Organization.

57. Leboyer, one of France's most respected pediatricians, urged that parents protect the newborn from a tendency of many birth attendants to aggressively and prematurely separate the infant from his umbilical blood. He writes: "So at all costs, the child must not lack oxygen at birth, not even for an instant. . . . Two systems function simultaneously, one relieving the other, the old one, the umbilicus, continues to supply oxygen to the baby until the new one, the lungs, has fully taken its place. Oxygenated by the umbilicus, protected from anoxia, the baby can settle into breathing without danger and without shock, unhurried and in its own time. In addition, the blood has plenty of time to abandon its old route (which leads to the placenta) and progressively fill the pulmonary system. During this period, moreover, an orifice closes to the heart, which seals off the old route for ever (sic) . . . . In short, for an average of four or five minutes, the newborn infant straddles two worlds. Drawing oxygen from two sources, it switches gradually from one to the other without the brutal transition, with hardly a cry. . . . If the cord is severed as soon as the baby is born, the baby's brain is brutally deprived of oxygen . . . The baby's alarm system is thus alerted and the baby's entire organism reacts. Everything in the body language of the child . . . the frenzied agitation of its limbs, the very tone of its cries . . . expresses the immensity of its panic, and its effort to escape. (p. 44, 45)." Could many of the disabilities afflicting children world-wide such as blindness, epilepsy, cerebral palsy, mental retardation, etc., be attributable, in part, to birth attendants' failure to follow Leboyer's common-sense advice?

22

SUCK THE THROAT CLEAR

THE WAY FOR AIR must be cleared before the newborn can breathe on his own. Holding the newborn upside down is one way of clearing the air passageway. But that is a humiliating way, which is upsetting to the entire organism.

There are better ways of clearing the air passageway. Fortunately, most modern hospitals have gentle suction devices that can clear the newborn's nostrils and throat very painlessly and quickly. This is sometimes followed by a gentle kiss on the lips from the mother that provokes a sucking reflex which, in turn, reinforces the infant's natural efforts to draw in air. Such procedures are a pleasant first contact with the skin of another human. From such contacts the newborn learns that this is not such a bad world after all and that it is probably interesting and worth finding out about.

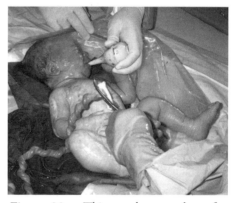

Figure 23. This newborn, only a few moments after birth, has begun to relax. Notice that most of the distress of birth has disappeared from his face. A suction syringe is being used here to clear his breathing passages. Before the introduction of the suction syringe, most cultures encouraged the mother to suck the infant's mouth and throat clear, or the midwife would do so. Turning the baby upside down to clear his air passages is cruel and unnecessary.

The newborn child so introduced to the world is more likely to want to affiliate with such a world than the child whose initiation is harsher. We must begin to see the intellect as both inborn, that is, determined by one's genes *and* a result of how one is treated by the world. First impressions are usually rather lasting.

23

DON'T SPANK

EIGHTEENTH CENTURY PHYSICIANS got into the habit of spanking the newborn. How did this practice arise? We can assure the reader that no midwife would ever condone this practice. But, breathing is almost automatic with the combinations of gravity, a cleared throat, and the rush of air around the face. The contrast between the womb and this external world is so great to the newborn as to stimulate the gasp of surprise by the infant, who by reflex action automatically sucks in air.

There are better ways than spanking!

Instead of spanking, if the infant does not start breathing, try a little artificial respiration, that is, massaging the chest cavity. Ancient Polynesian and Micronesian cultures routinely massaged the newborn anyway so as to establish for it the proper breathing rhythms. Some families still practice that gentle and loving art.

Figure 24. There are several alternatives to spanking depending on the circumstance. At birth, the alternative to spanking is the suction syringe. Later in the infant's rapid development, an alternative is a hug.

BREATHING IS THE INFANT'S FIRST REAL TASTE OF INDEPENDENCE.

If the infant learns – yes, learns – to breathe on its own, it will have taught itself a vital lesson, valuable throughout its life: his survival in and his ultimate mastery of this world depends upon his own independent effort. People with high intelligence are fortunate enough to have been allowed to discover that they must act upon their environment; that they must not be passive reactors to the environment.

We advise letting the baby teach himself to breathe. Don't impatiently force breathing upon him and he will ecstatically enjoy that learning experience. The warm, natural air will taste good to him. It is his first taste of this world. Let it be pleasant. Let the child learn in that powerfully sensitive moment that while life may have some anxieties and pains, the first moments are intended to be exquisitely pleasant.[58]

---

58. Spanking, for whatever reason, is considered child abuse in the Scandinavian countries and other nations and is punishable by a fine or imprisonment. Those nations passed such legislation based upon sound research. The research and the writings of Lamaze and Leboyer since the 1930s and 1940s have demonstrated that spanking the newborn to stimulate breathing is painful and unnecessary.

For a summary of the entire topic of child abuse worldwide see Neil Gilbert (Ed.), *Combating Child Abuse: International Perspectives and Trends*. New York and Oxford: Oxford University Press. 1997

Part V
Some Specific Suggestions
for Immediately after Birth
and the First Year

24

BATHE GENTLY

ONE OF THE FIRST and most important experiences that a mother shares with the newborn is the first bath.

Warm, pure, clear water comforts and reassures the newborn that this world is as protective and loving as the one he has just left behind.

The mother will intuitively handle the baby gently, firmly, and safely. All items necessary for the bath, including the wash cloths and towels, are organized and at her fingertips for this pleasant, basic, and loving procedure. The bath is as necessary as the feeding experience and it should become as regular, almost as a ritual.

The purpose of the bath is, of course, cleanliness of the body which is a pre-requisite for good health. The bath also provides the mother an opportunity to inspect her infant's body for any sign of infection or damage.

Figure 25. "Hey, Mom, don't scare me." Human beings are frightened of new experiences, even when that new experience is with a trusted parent. Once bathing is experienced, with the right temperature, of course, the baby will enjoy being bathed. This mother decided to reduce the danger of drowning by placing the baby in a bucket rather than a tub.

The bathing time also provides the mother and baby a daily opportunity to commune together, to have intimate contact, to study each other's eyes and facial expressions and to deepen the bond that exists between them.

The bathing time is bonding time, is renewal time and a gentle reminder that cleanliness is a daily necessity. The infant will gradually make the necessary transfer of learning, from the physical to the mental: as he learned to expect the daily bath, so will he learn to expect other events that will cleanse his mind and his spirit.[59]

---

59. Erik Erikson, in his classic, *Childhood and Society*, proposed that the child's world view, or basic philosophy of life is summed up in her question: "Is the Universe sensitive to my needs?" The child's answer (to her own question) is determined largely by the nature of the mother's hour-by-hour treatment of the child. Erikson frequently urged "gentle movements of the mother" when dealing with the infant.

25

LET THE MOTHER CUDDLE THE INFANT IMMEDIATELY

YES, THE MOTHER is tired after birth and exhausted. So is the infant. He, too, struggled with considerable pain to crawl through the birth canal. Both have not only exhausted themselves, but have achieved one of the world's great victories: a successful birth of a new soul into this earthly life. Let them celebrate together, even if only for a few seconds in each other's arms and, like two tired victorious warriors, enjoy the ecstasy of victory and of having narrowly escaped from the jaws of defeat.

Figure 26. Babies have several fears. The most frightening is the thought of losing mother. Therefore midwives and good hospitals never separate the baby from the mother, except in extreme circumstances.

After the infant is briefly cleaned and after the mother is cleaned and all the blood disposed of, let them relax on new clean, dry sheets – together. The emotional satisfaction is surely one of the richest of all human experiences and should be enjoyed to the fullest.

Then, let them sleep close together, skin to skin. The mother's acutely trained and sensitive reflexes will prevent her from rolling over on or smothering her newborn.

We wonder where the fear that the mother might crush her own infant came from? In normally healthy humans, such fears are groundless.

Sleeping close to the mother, the infant, now beginning to exercise some controls over both the so-called "voluntary" muscles and the "involuntary" muscles, will almost intuitively harmonize his heart-beat with his mother's and his breathing rate with hers. In those delicious moments of nearness, the new human learns the pleasure of telling his heart and his respiratory muscles, "Harmonize yourselves with drumbeats of the universe, the drumbeats set by my mother."

Thus cuddling and sleeping not only provide emotional reassurance, they provide an opportunity for the child to learn the basic rhythms of the universe in a new context, that there is a continuity of life from within the womb to without. Life, this now thinking human tells itself, is of one seamless cord, a cord of rhythm, "to which have clung all in this world and in the world to come."[60]

---

60. The mother normally is not physically capable of taking care of her infant alone. She wants to cuddle the newborn, but she is thinking of dozens of tasks. T. Berry Brazelton wrote, "When I studied the Mayan Indians in Southern Mexico for their early child rearing patterns, I longed for the revival in our society of at least two customs that we as a culture have given up. I longed for the mothers to allow themselves more continual physical closeness with their infants and for the cushioning of the extended family for all young parents. . . other cultures emphasize the extended family as a source of strength and direction." (1983, p.xxv)

26

FEED COLOSTRUM TO THE INFANT AND BREAST-FEED

COLOSTRUM IS AVAILABLE at this time only from the mother's breast.[61] No one has been able to imitate this amazing liquid produced by the mother's body.

Colostrum, which is not milk, appears to have been extraordinarily well-designed by nature to start the infant off on a healthy life. It contains many diverse substances, some of whose roles are still not understood by physiologists. Those, which are partly understood, include:

— Multinucleated cells, "loaded with particles of fat." Obviously the fat will quickly turn into energy and help spark an appetite, as well as alertness and growth.

— Lactalbumin, which is a protein. Apparently, this particular protein can quickly participate in the process of building new tissue for

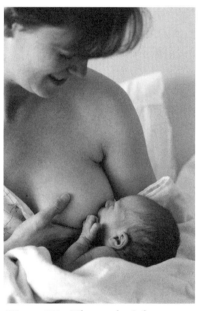

Figure 27. The mother's breasts are incredible chemical factories. The breasts' first production is colostrum. Then each subsequent feeding is tailor-made for her infant.

---

61. Normally, colostrum is available only on the first feeding.

the infant. In contrast to its ability to manufacture certain nutrients, the body cannot manufacture protein for the building of tissue. It must use protein from food but, obviously, the baby's body is not ready for the "heavier" proteins, not even for some of the proteins in its mother's milk.

— Lactoglobulin, another protein – this one not soluble in water. It is speculated that this protein carries several antibodies to enable the infant to fight off germs that he will quickly encounter in the environment.

— Inorganic salts. The baby's body will use these in a variety of ways: to build bone tissue, blood cells, brain tissue, etc.

Mothers should understand that colostrum is not milk. It differs from milk in several important ways. For example, colostrum contains little or no caseinogen which is a major component of milk.

In addition to helping the infant's body get off to a good physical start, colostrum has a laxative effect on the newborn, cleaning out his digestive tract and preparing it for a kind of food that he has never experienced before.

We infer a philosophical principle of the universe here: each experience in life should have a forerunner. Death should be preceded by dreams or visions and to the infant, extra-uterine life is foreshadowed by sounds and changes in the mother's position and, finally, by dimly perceived light. The forerunner of all food is colostrum.

Even if the mother chooses not to breast-feed, she should, unless she has cancer or unless some other powerful force is operating in her body, at least give her baby its first food, colostrum.

But she should breast-feed. The World Health Organization published in 1977 a handbook on infant care that strongly recommends breast-feeding. That handbook lists more than 50 good reasons to breast-feed. Some of those reasons are common-sense; desirable from several kinds of perspectives, including from the perspectives of tradition, of intuition, and of modern research findings:[62]

— Mother's milk is *tailor-made* for her infant. Human milk is very different from cow's milk. For example, the human mother's milk contains about 30% to 40% more sugar than cow's milk. Consequently, makers of artificial formulas have to add extra, "unnatural" sugar – sugar that is unnatural to the infant. Often, the infant fed such artificially sweetened milk become hyperactive, flighty.

— Mother's milk changes every time the infant feeds. The infant's saliva is absorbed by the mother's nipple. The mother's body then biochemically analyzes the saliva and all the germs and other messages that it contains and makes fine adjustments in the composition of the next output of milk. If the infant is getting too much fat, her milk is sensitively adjusted accordingly. If a particular germ has attacked the infant, her antibody building mechanisms go to work. In a few hours, her antibodies are transmitted to the infant via her milk and before the baby even knows that the germs are there, the mother's body has them under control.[63]

— At each feeding, the mother gives her infant 100,000 or so red blood cells from her body. So in each feeding, the infant is obtaining freshly made new proteins, in the form of his mother's red-blood cells. But the newborn is also receiving on the surface of those red blood cells the proper antibodies that she herself cannot yet manufacture.

— It is emotionally satisfying for mother and baby to share the breast-feeding experience. It strengthens the bond between them and strengthens the ability of both to bond with other humans. The emotional security of that bond then facilitates all other forms of growth, intellectual as well as emotional.

---

62. The World Health Organization has consistently recommended that mother's breast-feed, especially immediately after birth when colostrum is present. (Private communication from the World Health Organization, Geneva Switzerland, June 9, 2005. See also WHO references, page 168.)

63. For a fuller discussion of the advantages of breast-feeding visit La Leche League websites (www.lalecheleague.com). See also the WHO publications on breast feeding.

27

BOTH MOTHER AND FATHER TO SLEEP WITH THE BABY

SOME SOCIETIES TEND to isolate the infant. As soon as he born he is whisked off to a nursery with other babies and after arriving home sleeps in a separate room. Other societies, separate the mother and infant from the father after birth. For example, in some West African countries the mother and baby sleep in one house and the father in another house.

In our view, baby, mother, and father should form a stable triangle, the fundamental social building block, and the matrix in which the basic grammars of human relationships are learned. This triangle, baby, mother and father, should be formed at the moment of delivery and be encouraged to flourish within the context of intimate family life.

Figure 28. The family bed is as old as mankind. The Polynesian custom was dad next to the wall, then mom, then the youngest child, then the next oldest child, etc. When the child reached age six he or she was expected to go into another bed.

Many cultures justify separating the father from the baby on grounds that the baby might be smothered in the family bed. However, we know of no documented case where a parent has accidentally smothered an infant in the family bed.

There are emotional advantages for the infant who sleeps with both parents. One of the most obvious is that when the baby sleeps in proximity to at least one of his parents his nightmares dissipate quickly. His sleep is deeper and his breathing rhythms more mature. Moreover, while most babies learn to breathe almost automatically, other babies require a degree of learning, using the parents as models. In effect, some babies need a breathing coach; they need to learn the proper rhythms of breathing lest they sometimes forget to breathe. Incidentally, apparently in harmony with the laws of sociobiology, all primates, except some human tribes and cultures, sleep with their infants until the end of "early childhood."[64] Our review of recent research studies dealing with family sleeping patterns compels us to recommend that all families reconsider the historically recent practice of isolating the newborn. We believe the healthiest practice is for parents to resurrect the family bed.

---

64. For a discussion of the advantages of the family bed, see *Nighttime Parenting: How to Get Your Baby and Child* to Sleep by William M.D. Sears (La Leche League International, Schaumberg, IL). Parents who wish to further explore this topic may consult the parenting blog At*tachment Parenting*, (www.apparenting.com) or similar websites for informative discussions of the "family bed" or "co-sleeping" patterns.

28

MOTHER AND FATHER TO AVOID SEX IN BABY'S PRESENCE

SEX, WITH MOST adults is a vigorous activity. To an infant, it sometimes appears loud. Vigorous motions, strange noises frighten an infant, especially if his mother is involved. The infant obviously interprets this vigorous action as violent action, harmful action.

Many societies, using common sense, publish taboos against sex in the presence of the child, lest the child misunderstand and, particularly, lest the child learn early to think of the male in the house as the person who harms his mother.

It is our observation that in those societies where the infant is a frequent witness to the sex act involving his mother, such children often have difficulty in developing a strong bond with their fathers or any other male authority figure.[65, 66]

Societies in which these feelings of estrangement are widespread will, from our observations, be difficult to govern, except through recourse to violence, that is, except through dictatorships.

In a climate of violence, rational, problem-solving intelligence diminishes.

---

65. In Polynesia where the family bed is still customary, the mother and father find a place other than the family bed for sex.

66. Melville Herskovitz in Hsu (1961) reports on the family dynamics which produce not only estrangement between child and father, but also between child and child.

29

TRAIN THE INFANT'S SENSES

BORN IN DARKNESS — ideally — the infant's early fascinations are with her newfound sense perceptions. She is beginning to experience a new and exciting universe. If that experience is overwhelming (too cold, too bright, too loud, too rough, too smelly, or too bitter) the child's natural, animal-like response is to retreat. That is, "rough" or "harsh" or other unattractive aspects of an infant's environment, such as a cold stethoscope or clumsily handled suction device can

Figure 29. What do babies think about? The first question the baby asks is, "Am I loved? Does the universe love me?"

cause her to fear her new environment. Newborns have several built-in fears, loud sounds, for example, which if activated, cause some neural connections to "shut down," in effect, retarding the development of the infant's brain. (There have been several definitive experiments that have shown that either excessive exposure or under-exposure to stimuli may cause certain nerves associated with those sensations to wither.)[67]

Parents then, will obviously wish to be sensitive to the effects that stimuli in the child's environment will have upon the child's neurons (brain cells) that respond to those stimuli. Some neurons connect to 10,000 others. The process of building networks in the brain begins before birth and

---

67. For example, blindfolded cats lose the function of the optic nerves; teen-agers exposed to loud music lose hearing acuity, etc.

accelerates for the first two years of life and continues throughout life. Our recommendations:

LIGHT: Very gentle at first, then pale colors.

SOUND: The mother's gentle voice against a quiet background is recommended. (Some tribes still isolate the mother from all noise several weeks before birth. Nearly all tribal villages with which we are familiar used to ban loud ceremonies near new infants, especially "high-born" infants.)[68]

TASTE: The ideal taste for the infant is mother's milk which changes in taste automatically to alert the infant that different tastes exist. As the mother's foods change, so will the taste of her milk. Sensitive mothers will of course avoid extreme tastes such as raw onions or quinine-flavored drinks or alcohol, etc. Incidentally, infants hate the taste of alcohol, and beer is repulsive to them.

SMELL: The infant's olfactory senses, of course, begin to function soon after birth. "Clean" scents are recommended; "heavy" scents should be avoided. In the Middle East in ancient times it was customary to give newborns mild fragrances such as frankincense and myrrh. Some East Indian societies, especially the upper classes, retain this custom even to this day, obviously to train the infant's sense of smell. Such gift-bringers know that occasionally one's well-being depends upon having an "educated" nose.

---

68. Suzuki, who invented a pedagogy for musical training, recommends that ear training begin at or near age two. Training all five senses is such a new area of infant and child education that the parents should make a game of finding how best to do it at each developmental stage.

30

HELP THE INFANT TRAIN ITS SENSE OF BALANCE

IN "THE GREEN LIGHT EXPEDITION," a full-length film of a remote Amazon region, the producer, Madam Rúhíyyih Khanum of Haifa, Israel, showed an unforgettable and charming scene: an Indian girl, perhaps four of five years old swinging her younger brother or sister in a handmade basket swing.

Figure 30.   Children have five basic fears, including the fear of falling. A well-trained sense of balance counteracts that particular fear.

All known human cultures swing or rock or cradle their infants. The reasons for this are many. One is to train the infant early to orient itself in space by skillfully interpreting all of its psychomotor sensations. This skillful interpreting comes about through training. The potential is inborn or innate, but the potential can only be realized through training.

Cats train their young by carrying them about, back feet down. An athlete or dancer who moves with "cat-like grace" had his/her sense of balance educated early. His/her father tossed him/her about at the important developmental periods: a tiny bit at three months, more vigorously at six months, and delightful "horseplay" at 18 months.

Mary Lou Retton, the 1984 Olympic Gymnastics gold-medal winner, explains that from the time of her earliest memories she enjoyed being tossed about and tossing herself about the family living-room couch.

This point is supported in hundreds of research studies. One of the most interesting is cited by Howard Gardner of Harvard University:

> "And what of the development links between a child's early preoccupations and eventual inventiveness in a highly valued contemporary occupation like engineering? An intriguing set of clues can be found in Tracy Kidder's account of those 'whiz-kids' who build new computer hardware. In the case of several of these talented inventors, much time during childhood was spent in the taking apart of mechanical objects. Describing one such worker, Kidder notes: 'Like practically everyone else on the team, he started becoming an engineer at about age four . . .' (p. 233)

The sense of balance is a part of what Howard Gardner calls the "Bodily-Kinesthetic Intelligence", which must be possessed in high quantities by the professional dancer, the actor, the athlete and the inventive engineer. Skills in this area must also be high, of course, in the surgeon, the dentist, the architect, anyone who works in three dimensions.

The sense of balance is also central to what Gardner calls the "spatial intelligence".[69, 70]

---

69. See Howard Gardner, *Frames of Mind: The Theory of Multiple Intelligences.* New York: Basic Books, 1973.

70. Why do certain North American Indian tribes dominate the high-rise steel-frame construction trade on the East Coast? This, too, is a new area of potentially fertile research. Losing the fear of heights is a consequence of parents allowing the child the freedom to explore climbing activities. But the loss of the fear of heights probably occurs at some very early "sensitive moment" — a term that Montessori borrowed from biologists concerned with the often very narrow developmental window within organisms. Biologists and Montessori recognized that appropriate developmental changes occur only if the appropriate stimuli are present.

31

BEGIN EAR TRAINING

Figure 31. Plato, considered by many as being among the world's greatest educationists – he taught Aristotle after having been taught by Socrates – strongly suggested music as an integral element of school curricula. He also justified mathematics as "making a strong mind quick". Plato also noted that young children who undergo physical-education training perform better as scholars.

PARENTS ALMOST INTUITIVELY will begin ear-training early, but it should be done with some expertness.

"Baby-talk," that peculiar set of sounds adults direct to infants, is not without reason: the voice is softened and includes no harsh aspirant or nasal or guttural sounds. We, in English, do not say "good," emphasizing the "d." We say "goo-goo." We do not say, "to bed," pronouncing the "d" carefully. We say "to beddy-bye," softening the "d." We do not say "hush." We say "shsh," etc.

Parents who talk to the infant will note that at first, the infant pays attention to (by inference prefers) the mother's voice. But after several weeks the infant will give more attention to the male voice.

Gentle music, of course, trains the ear, or, more accurately, gives the infant the experiences to train its own ear. And, of course, music for infants soothes their untrained emotions. All the fifty cultures that we have experienced have lovely lullabies for infants and children.

One reason that many African children have such a developed sense of rhythm is that their parents wisely begin this training very early. From about 60 to 100 days after birth, the infant is taken to village festivals where the infant's legs and arms are moved by the mother or by the other children to the rhythms of the festival in a joyful and playful manner. The learning accelerates from that moment.

A reason that musicians and all the rest of us can look forward to a more beautiful aural future is that all parents will be sensitive to the need to begin ear-training (different rhythms, different tones) very soon after birth.

Figure 32. The best-known ear-training instruments are the mother's modulated voice and stringed or wind instruments playing baroque music. As they develop, the musically sensitive parts of the brain demand other sounds.

32

WEAN GENTLY

MOST PEOPLE THINK of the weaning period as a most difficult time for the infant.

This is not necessarily so.

A Tongan lady whom we know and who lives in Fiji assured us that her first child began refusing her breast milk at about six months.[71] Dr. Maria Montessori alerted us to expect such developmental cues or signals, but we had never run across such an actual case before, nor were we able to locate any ethnographical verification of such spontaneous weaning by babies.

We suspect, nevertheless, that if the mother is very sensitive to the child's maturing moods, she will discover that sometime around five months and possibly around eight months, the baby will actually express by body language that it wishes

Figure 33. Children who feel loved and secure actually attempt to wean themselves, perhaps as early as five months. Ideally, at or before 12 months.

---

71. Dr. Konai Thaman, Head, School of Education, University of the South Pacific, Suva, Fiji, in a personal interview, 1983. While such spontaneous weaning is rare in most cultures, it is well-known in Polynesian societies, according to Dr. Thaman.

to wean itself, just as it often sends a signal that it prefers to sleep alone at about the same age.[72, 73]

Although Dr. T. Berry Brazelton (in his *Infants and Mothers*) finds some justification to continue breast-feeding into the second or third year, especially in countries where nutritional levels are low and disease rates are high, having observed weaning practices in several cultures we suspect that to breast-feed an infant beyond nine or 12 months retards his or her evolution out of infancy.

One way of making the weaning a memorable event and less painful for the infant was given in Genesis: "And the child grew and was weaned: and Abraham made a great feast the same day that Isaac was weaned." This custom later evolved into the first birthday party for the child.

The important point of this lesson is that the emotions and the intellect are deeply interrelated. When one is depressed, the intellect does not function well. Similarly, if the intellect is impaired, emotional flexibility will be missing. A gentle weaning, perhaps combined with a happy event, will smooth the transition from one level of dependence to a new level of independence, a pattern that underlies all intellectual achievements.

---

72. At certain maturational stages, the child develops a temporary aversion to its mother's milk. We cannot predict precisely when that aversion will occur. All we can do is alert the mother that it will happen sometime between the fifth and the twelfth months. If the child continues to breast-feed through that temporary aversion period, the child then will become addicted to breast-feeding (not only to the mother's milk but to the comfort and safety that closeness to the mother provides) and weaning will be very painful for the child.

73. Additional discussion of the issues of weaning may be found on many websites, including the British Medical Journals (www.bmjjournals.com).

33

EXPOSE THE CHILD TO A WIDE CIRCLE OF AFFECTIONS

JEAN PIAGET, THE SWISS psychologist and arguably the most influential developmental psychologist of the 20th century, verbally drew for us a most useful mental image: the evolving self, continually expanding to unite with a concentric set of circles of relationships: self plus mother; then self plus mother and father; then self plus mother and father and siblings; then to the clan; to the nation, then to the race. And, we can extrapolate, finally to mankind as a whole.

Figure 34. A very powerful stimulus to the child to extend her circle of affections is the family reunion. Here one meets one's aunts, uncles, grandparents, cousins, etc. The atmosphere of affection in such reunions assists the child to embrace increasingly larger unities.

We think that the parents' role is simply to allow that "natural" growth to occur. We are not sure, and the evidence is not yet available and analyzed as to the "right" timing. The Korean culture, for example, traditionally said, "No visitors to the baby's home until after 100 days after the birth." Other cultures allow near relatives to visit the baby even after a few hours. The developmental principle that we are advocating is not to overwhelm the child with too many and too diverse stimuli. There is much room here for research as to the "ideal" sequencing of stimuli.

We recommend that parents thoughtfully examine the pattern prevailing in their culture and either follow it or modify it to fit their own intuitive feelings of what is right for their child. A pattern such as the one below may be helpful in reaching such a decision:

0 – 24 hours	Mother, mid-wife (or physician) only. Mainly, only mother. Father observes at a distance. (This allows the infant time to learn its mother's characteristics, before having to learn others'.)
1 – 3 days	Mother and her primary helpers (perhaps the mother's mother and aunt) and the father only. Father totally silent.
3 – 21 days	Siblings, female near relatives. Any near relatives may see, but only mother and adult female relatives may handle.
22 – 99 days	Family members only, all to be quiet.
100 days	The Koreans recommend a ceremony at 100 days: Extended family, but at a distance; also members of the same religion at a worship or public naming service.
101 days – 6 years	Gradually introduce the child to all varieties of mankind in a warm and accepting (non-biased) natural context or manner: members of different nationalities and ethnicities; and those in a variety of conditions, the poor, the wealthy, the athletic, and those who might have some physical handicap, etc.

The child should be taught, in a variety of ways, to respect and not to fear any of mankind's diversity, except, of course, those who pose a danger to society. It is human nature to fear those who are unknown or "strange" and it is also human nature not to fear that which is familiar. Fearlessness, typically, is a pre-requisite to high achievement in all human endeavors and is, therefore, to be encouraged. Obviously there are hundreds of ways to teach this trait. We are recommending the most natural ways.[74]

---

74. Gordon Allport (1979) at Harvard also verbally drew a set of concentric circles to indicate the child's ever-expanding circles of loyalty.

Baby plus mother

Baby plus mother plus father

Baby plus mother plus father plus siblings and extended family

Baby plus family plus clan

Baby plus clan plus tribe

Baby plus tribe plus nation

Baby plus nation plus race

Baby plus race plus all mankind

The developmental sequence described by Allport obviously is not automatic. If it were, there would be no national or racial or tribal prejudice, no oedipal conflicts in our world. It therefore follows that the parents must structure some experiences for the child so as to facilitate this natural psychological development.

34

KEEP THE INFANT CLEAN

DARWIN DISTINGUISHED the savage from civilized man by several qualities: absence of government, suspicion of strangers, and filthiness.

Cleanliness is a characteristic of noble people. We have seen mothers take a rag, wash the toilet, then use the same rag to wash the baby's face!

Such poor hygienic behavior nearly always subjects the baby to disease and the potential of low-level functioning. The mind cannot operate properly if the body is burdened with disease.

Intelligent mothers use different washcloths for the toilet, for the kitchen, and for the bathroom. Many wise mothers have forbidden the different cloths to be used for the other purposes. Indeed, some mothers have different cloths even for different parts of the infant's body.

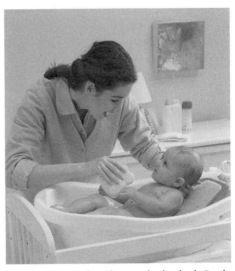

Figure 35. Babies love to be bathed. Bathing time is another opportunity for bonding. Of course, caretakers must use the mildest possible soaps and shampoos and be very deliberate and careful. Even adults hurt when they get soap in their eyes and can become angry. We must exert every effort to prevent anger in the child, for it is that unresolved anger that yields aggressive or deviant behaviors.

She does this for good reasons. The infant's face cloth is used only on his face because even a drop of his feces, even when unseen, can cause sores on his face.

Many northern European cultures literally considered "cleanliness next to Godliness." And all high cultures have some ritualistic practices to reinforce cleanliness: bathing in a clean river, washing with holy water, or even fasting to purify the body.

Keeping the infant physically clean is teaching him that there are diseases in the world that must be avoided, that he is always vulnerable, and that all humans must, as a life principle, take some precautions to prevent disease. Hopefully, the child will then one day make the transfer or analogy between his body, his mind, and his spirit. The clean infant learns to love cleanliness and to abhor dirtiness in any form.

Part VI
Some Specific Suggestions
From Year One

35
NAME THINGS FOR INFANTS

THE OLD TESTAMENT AND PSYCHOLOGICAL science agree: mankind was given dominion "over the fish of the sea, and over the fowl of the air, and over the cattle, and over the earth, and over every creeping thing that creepeth upon the earth."

To consolidate that dominion, Adam was instructed to give "names to all cattle, and to the fowl of the air, and to every beast of the field."

Carl Jung saw the symbol of naming things: it represents the establishing of a relationship with the thing named. Seen another way, if one does not know the name of a thing, one has not even started to learn about that thing.

One reason that writers in the Enlightenment (18th-Century European) Period admired many aspects of non-European cultures was that members of many of those cultures often knew the names of most plants, animals, and inanimate objects in their environment, to a greater degree than those in the European cultures. For example, the typical Polynesian islander had more than a dozen names for different sorts of ocean waves, or Eskimos had more than 30 names for snow. To know the name of a particular bird implied an educated sense of discrimination which, in turn, implied that one knew the value or habits or "omens" conveyed by the bird or object named. The appearance of a certain species of bird meant the beginning or ending of a season, a time to plant or a time to harvest, etc. If one knew the name, one knew more than the name.

Clever children, then, usually will have learned the names of most creatures and objects in their environment, if for no better reason than to demonstrate intelligence. Children who do not know the names of things look upon themselves as unintelligent, and their intelligence gradually diminishes.

One may test this by asking a child, "What is the name of your principal?" If the child can answer, more than an answer comes forth; a signal comes forth from the child: "See, I do listen and remember. I use my head." If the child cannot answer, and knows that he ought to be able to answer, an opposite expression crosses his face.

Figure 36.   Intelligence must frequently be reaffirmed.

Because of the ancient and modern significance of naming, we recommend that parents set some goals for their child. By the age of three years, this child will know:

— The names of all of its immediate family members.

— The names of all living grandparents.

— The names of the child's street, district, city.

— The names of its favorite foods.

— The names of all major plants inside the house.

— The names of any animals living in the immediate household or on the farm.

We recommend that similar goals be set for the child at age four, etc.

Intelligence is an ever-growing fragile construct that must be frequently refreshed, reaffirmed and augmented in the child in many different ways. The child must sense the necessity very early in her life that her intelligence must continue to grow.

36
LET THE CHILD NAME THINGS

THE PERCEPTIVE STUDENT of culture knows that many pedagogical lessons are taught by the great disciplines of mankind. For example, biology became a science only after Carl Linnaeus established a classification system for plants and animals. Dmitriy Mendeleev created the Periodic Table of the Elements, thus advancing the science of chemistry. And according to Jewish tradition, Adam named the creatures of the earth.

Figure 37. Maria Montessori insisted that the child wishes to learn the name of everything in her environment. If practiced regularly, this naming of objects and animals is not a chore. It is a kind of game.

The attentive parent, learning a lesson from those facts, will therefore find some way to let the child name things: a kitten, a puppy, a fish, a room, a stuffed toy, a section of the garden, even a game, or a piece of sand sculpture. So important is this principle that Maria Montessori recommended labeling almost everything in the child's environment until the child learns their names.

The process of naming makes a connection within part of the brain's or mind's feedback loop. Each newly discovered comet or planet is named by or after its discoverer. Similarly, when biologists discover a new species, they are given the honor of naming that species. That tradition of scientists naming things has a valid reason. Naming things gives one pleasure. And searching for new things to name spurs on the advancement of science. All benefit.

This naming process is a marvelous prescription for how to cultivate genius: encourage the child "to complete" the act of creation.[75] Little children from age two years will love to "complete" their father's or their mother's work:

— The father saws the legs for a stool. But the child sandpapers those legs.

— The father starts a row of beans, the child puts in the stakes and later trains the vines.

— The mother measures the ingredients for a batch of cookies, but the daughter does the stirring and the pouring.

This list could be endlessly extended.

After completing the task the child then does not feel patronized by being given the honor of naming the "completed" object.

Every highly intelligent person whose life we have studied appears to have been so inducted into the world of creative intellect. And such induction must start early, so that the creative impulses become a stronger part of the unconscious, a very powerful part of the mind.[76]

---

75. Evolutionary biologists are beginning to question who first domesticated animals. Isaac Asimov, the biochemist and science fiction writer, wrote that it may have been children, who can bond across species must faster than adults and who have a built-in desire to name everything significant to them (1994).

76. This concept was taught by most of the founders of the various schools of psychology, Freud, Jung, Erikson, etc.

37

ASSIST THE CHILD TO MASTER LANGUAGE

GEORGE BERNARD SHAW was right in his play, "Pygmalion," which many saw in its musical translation, "My Fair Lady": a person's language does not necessarily convey a person's intelligence. But a person's language is a powerful tool for enhancing the quality of his life.

All humans now live in a mobile or fluid society, a society in which a person's opportunities for success are determined less by his inheritance and more by his achievements. Therefore, wise parents will train their children in all the skills and nuances of language.

Figure 38. "And God taught man articulate speech" is a recurring refrain in the Holy Koran. "In the beginning was the Word . . ." is a Christian theme, indicating the status of language in the universe. "Through us the universe speaks with itself" is a line in a poem by Nobel Literature Prize Winner Octavio Paz. Thus, all cultures urge good parents to give great emphasis to language learning.

The mobility or fluidity of world societies is easily demonstrated by the "brain drain." One report some years ago in *West Africa* magazine said that one-half of Ivorian (natives of the Ivory Coast) physicians were practicing in France. In the original statistics section of the Research Triangle Institute in North Carolina Governor Terry Sanford's brilliant idea for a Research Triangle Park, five of the six statisticians – hand-picked from the top applicants in the world – were Indian nationals trained in the United States. A visit to any first-class academic or high-technology department anywhere in the world reveals a similar pattern: talented people keep moving.

View the situation from the employer's perspective. For example, an employer offering a top position, whether it is a statistician or a policy analyst or a professor of physics, has from 50 to 200 or more applicants. Who is she going to hire? After the search committee screens down to six or eight well-qualified candidates, the cutting edge goes to the candidate who is able to hold his own in intelligent conversation. The interview, a natural part of any selective process, favors the candidate whose parents trained him to respect and use the language well.

From the beginning, from birth, and until they die, humans experience some difficulty with language. (This, plus the fact that most humans actually master their language by age six, provided the primary proof for Dr. Claude Levi-Strauss to assert that all humans are geniuses and "have been so for at least a million years.")[77]

One of the first clear sentences that American middle-class babies utter is "All gone!", to confirm to their mothers that they have eaten all their food. But preceding the articulation of those words are some babble with the "all gone" intonation. Thus, we can infer that children "master" the *tones* of a language before they master the *words* of a language. Indeed, to a child, "all gone" sounds like one word. Therefore, clever mothers, beginning when their babies are around four or five months, start to articulate distinctly every single word when they are "conversing" with their infant.

Children will have difficulty through age three to five with polysyllabic words unless those polysyllables are repetitive such as "pee pee" or "bye-bye" or "*Rakiraki*". At certain stages, children love to demonstrate to their parent: "See! I have mastered polysyllabic words. Watch me say 'bye-bye' to Daddy or to Aunty."

And although the child will discover many puzzling language structures and rules – the past perfect tense, for example – the child, usually by age

---

77. Some students of human evolution have disputed Levi-Strauss' "million years" figure on the assumption that the larynx did not appear in our species until approximately 100,000 years ago, thus precluding articulate speech until then. We cannot recapture Levi-Strauss' reasoning process. However, we think that his counter argument would have been that sophisticated sign and body language would have emerged within our species more than a million years ago.

six, even where the parents do not speak the language perfectly, will have mastered most of the pronunciation and syntax problems of his or her language.

But it is the level of mastery that discriminates. In the future, we trust that all parents will be trained to spot any obstacle in the way of their child's mastery of the language and be able to take appropriate action.

For the normal child, the usual appropriate action is an educated example. The child is so smart that it will itself extract from that example all the right rules.

But occasionally, even the genius needs help.

There is more than sufficient evidence that children learn on their own, almost independently, or inductively, the grammar rules of their language by age six.

Children will use such words (in English) as

mouses	moneys
runned	singed (for sang)
hitted	gooder
goodest	eated

which indicates that they have used inductive logic to arrive at the "rules" whereby the English language expresses plurality or conjugates its verbs or inflects its adjectives. No one will necessarily have given the child a lecture on "tenses" or parts of speech inflections or the like. Similar examples exist in all natural languages to demonstrate that even in their "mistakes" children are manifesting a high order of learning skill.

All languages create those exceptions to the general rules and create subtle meaning shifts for which even the most clever child will have difficulty decoding or finding the general principle. In wise homes and villages, sensitive elders know when to allow the child to continue using "gooder" and when to advise the child to say "better."

In the above examples of words that do not follow the normal rule, there is no harm, probably, in allowing the child some freedom to discover the correct word on his own. But there is harm done if the parents are so insensitive to language as to speak so that the child can never figure out the rules of his language, or if the conversation is so sparse as not to provide enough instances for the child so that he can learn the rules.

Figure 39. The speech centers of the human brain contain hundreds of millions of neurons each one of which is capable of discriminating the most subtle sounds and in turn training voice and face muscles. Bronislaw Malinowski (1884-1942) pioneered in several fields. He taught mankind that for most people language learning begins with ear-training, then vocalization, then structuring simple sentences and ultimately grammatical analysis, not the other way around as was then customarily taught in schools.

The child whose language is retarded will always be at a relative disadvantage when communicating with children or adults who are verbally more agile or skillful.

How should parents help the child to develop its language abilities? The parents should use as many strategies as they can reasonably imagine: ask the child to tell his dream from the night before; narrate his visit to Grandma's; explain what happened when he visited the seashore; make up stories about where things came from; describe what he thinks the maker of some object looks like.

And, of course, one of the most universal techniques to teach the child grammar is to read to the child and then discuss the story.

Later, around age four and one-half or five years, the child will enjoy memorizing nursery rhymes, then poems, then short prayers.

By the age of six, a normal child should really have mastered almost every aspect of his language. After six years, for most children, language learning ceases to become pleasurable. Children evolve to want to learn "the message, not the medium of the message."

We have noticed that around the world, a large percentage of children begin to show boredom with school around the sixth grade. Perhaps one of the factors causing this boredom is the excessive didactic or direct emphasis upon language. Such direct approaches, to some degree, patronize the child's natural abilities to learn its language. Better, we feel, would be more substantive material. (Our favorite case to illustrate this was of a teen-age boy who was poor in reading and didn't like to read. The father bought him an old used automobile and a repair manual. The boy quickly learned to read well enough).

38

PARENTS TO AVOID BEHAVIOR THAT PRODUCES THE AUTOCRATIC PERSONALITY

CERTAIN FAMILIES IN ALL CULTURES produce children with very democratic behavior patterns. Other families set the conditions that produce the tyrant, the bully, the autocratic personality, the ego-centered person.[78]

The child raised in a manner favored by democratic societies will have the following interpersonal characteristics: the child will be considerate of the rights and feelings of others; will be courteous; and will be kind. The child who has the autocratic or authoritarian personality will demonstrate some of the following characteristics: likes to exercise absolute authority; demonstrates cruelty to animals and to weaker or younger persons; is prone to violence; pouts when unable to have own way, etc.

Where does a child acquire these opposite sets of qualities? The more negative and more animalistic qualities are built in. The more humane qualities are learned. A proper education considers both sets of qualities, the animal-like (territoriality, aggression, a

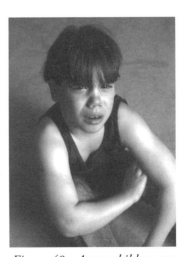

Figure 40. Angry children are dangerous, to themselves, to their families and to society. When does anger management begin? At birth. At every crisis, the child must learn that there is a solution, there is redemption, there are ways to cope. The best people in a position to teach anger management are skillful parents.

tendency to anger, etc.) and the humane (compassion, kindness, a sense of justice, etc.), as essentially positive, but requiring some transmutation. It is well-known among psychologists who deal with adolescents that children who have a good relationship with their fathers are unlikely to exhibit those negative qualities. We are not sure how over-aggressiveness, for example, is transmuted by a father's presence, but we know that that is one more reason for women to be careful in choosing a husband. She must choose a man who will stay with the family long enough to help with this difficult "identity" period, when the "independence drive" strongly asserts itself.

Children, almost from birth, will begin to assert their independence. And, independence is manifested by self-will. The child's "no" stage does not emerge at age two years, as some books allege. It is always there, but in different degrees. Aggression does not come at the "fighting" stage. It is always there, but at times under greater control than at other times. Wise, sophisticated and secure parents will allow their child great independence, tolerate many "no's"; accommodate and channel the child's natural aggressiveness.

But children have no built-in ethical or moral sense, no experience to tell them where the limits of their allowable behaviors lie. They will explore those limits, nearly all of those limits. The parents who allow their child to go too far, to demonstrate too much aggression, to hurt others with impunity, are preparing their child for a life of anger and frustration. The bully who hurts others is creating forces that will one day be reflected back upon himself. The adult world does not long tolerate grown-up self-willed children.

To avoid producing the autocratic or authoritarian personality, the parents should consider practicing the following:

Child's Age	Interpersonal Skills Training Strategy
0 – 2 years	Love, touch. Don't fear spoiling. Fulfill the child's first and greatest need: to be loved.

---

78. Erikson found that Adolph Hitler and Mahatma Gandhi were almost mirror images of each other in a scientific sense. Neither personality was a product of nature, but rather each personality was a product of parenting.

2 – 4 years	Set limits for the child, encourage the child's natural love for orderliness. Fulfill the child's need for affiliation by showing the child how it is related to its relatives and ultimately to all mankind.
5 – 7 years	Fulfill the child's now growing need to communicate: encourage a lot of intelligent conversation between child and adults. (Most dictators or autocrats were lonely children). Introduce child to both cooperative and competitive games.
7 – 11 years	Regularly play various sorts of games with the child, physical, social, and intellectual. Sensitively observe for any evidence that the child's interpersonal skills are out of focus and gently attempt to correct any such "flaw" *within* the game. (The child usually will make any necessary "transfer of learning" from the game to real life).

To learn in play is to learn in a non-threatening context. In some families, for example, the child hates to lose and becomes angry when he does. Games provide a powerful medium whereby the parent can detect that inappropriate response and correct it before it becomes a habit or characteristic).

Part VII
Some Specific Suggestions
From Age Two

39

INSIST UPON NEATNESS AND ORDER

SIGMUND FREUD speculated that a child grows through five stages corresponding with the parts of its body that then most interest it: the oral, anal, phallic, latency and genital.

We are not sure that those labels properly describe the child's primary focus or interest. But it is difficult to argue with Freud's general proposition that a child who is arrested in any one of those stages becomes an unattractive adult. If a child is arrested in the oral stage – that is, if the child is not encouraged to

Figure 41. At about age two, all children prefer order and neatness. If that quality of orderliness is reinforced and rewarded, it carries over into adolescence and adulthood. Ideally, the baby's crib should be in the family bedroom during the first two years of life to prevent nightmares and night terrors.

move into the so-called anal stage of neatness and self-control, the child will manifest one or more of the unpleasant attributes of the oral stage: gluttony, sloppiness and carelessness, passivity, etc. If a child is arrested in the anal stage he or she will be "tight" or "up-tight," stingy, uncommunicative, and overly pre-occupied with "everything in its place."

It is difficult to quarrel with the virtues usually learned in the so-called "anal" stage: love of order, of neatness, cleanliness, etc. The age at which these virtues are to be taught generally is around two years and, like most other "sensitive moments," will be a transient period.

Many geniuses are, of course, disorderly at times. But most people with high intelligence or high achievement drive feel uncomfortable in situations of disorder. When the love of order stage arrives in the child, the child will actually cooperate to make his environment orderly. He will gladly put away his toys, if the parents convey that expectation to him; he will gladly assume responsibility for some of the chores around the home, if encouraged to do so. (One reason that such helpfulness is not manifest in some homes is that the parents start expecting such helpfulness much too late.)

Unless the parents encourage this helpful and orderly spirit at the right time, the child will begin to assume that his mother is his servant and treat her accordingly – sometimes even with abuse.

It is in the realm of orderliness that the parents cannot afford to lose the almost endless set of battles of the egos. The child must know that his environment is ordered and that the parents are, in a sense, merely enforcing that order. They are not being spiteful of his disorder.

When a child appreciates that subtle point – and he can appreciate it more easily if the point is timed rightly – he is then ready for more profound lessons, such as the discipline inherent in learning to read, to write, to play musical instruments, to conduct research, etc.

40
ENCOURAGE THE CHILD TO SHARE

CHILDREN ARE, IN SOME sense, ego-centered. If that ego-centeredness persists, they will be considered "difficult persons" by their family and their peers.

The simplest way for parents to save their child from this unfortunate condition is to teach the child to share, insist that the child think of others, and come out of his ego-cocoon.

Figure 42. All the basic virtues underlying justice are learned in the home early in the life of the child. Sharing, empathy, fair play, must be explicitly taught, although the child has a natural inclination to these virtues at certain critical stages. Here the family is playing Kalah, one of mankind's oldest games and one probably played by Plato, who said that a primary vehicle for teaching justice is via play and games.

In some extended-family societies, such sharing and the pruning of the ego often happens automatically because of the social customs. In Samoa and Papua New Guinea, the four-year-old often watches over the two-year-old, thus losing some of his self-centeredness.

However, in some families in all societies, the child is sometimes alternately neglected, then over-indulged. Such inconsistent parental behavior also helps to produce a personality with an unstable ego, because it is not able to predict which of its behaviors bring reward and which bring punishment.

In sum: the parents who want their child to manifest a high intelligence and a high need for achievement must assist that child to have an integrated ego structure, a structure of integrity. One simple way of doing that is to consciously encourage the child to share, to worry about others, which most parents in all cultures do almost automatically. And the parents must reward that behavior and withhold reward for any selfish behavior. [79]

---

79. Howard Gardner (1983) suggests that the inter-personal skills are the most neglected intellectual skills and the ones that most urgently need to be taught deliberately in the home and in school. The door to inventiveness in this area is wide open.

41

TEACH THE CHILD HUMAN RELATIONSHIPS

PART OF INTELLIGENCE is the ability to perceive relationships between things or ideas where the relationship is not obvious. One of the major examinations for admission to graduate schools is the "Miller Analogies" test, an examination of nothing but analogical relationships. For example, house is to humans as nest is to birds.

Figure 43. Franz Boas, the Dane and father of American Anthropology, sent Margaret Mead to Samoa to study child development. Mead's findings revolutionized theories about human development. Sibling rivalry is not inevitable; adolescents don't necessarily rebel.

Children will independently arrive at an understanding of such relationships most quickly in the context of family. Young children, often around age three or four, will reason thus: "I am to my father as my father is to Grandpa." Or, "My father had the same relationship to his father as I have to him."

Such learning is often so effortless, so silent, that most parents are unaware that it is taking place. But perhaps it is wise to articulate some of those relationships for the child so that its intuitive understanding can inform its awakening verbal understanding:

"John, that was your father's father on the telephone, your grandfather."

"Mary, my grandmother, your great-grandmother, is coming for a visit."

"Peter, this is your Aunt Helen, your father's sister."

"Tomas, here comes your Aunt Maria with your cousin, Elena."

Names are not sufficient. Children have a need to know the person's relevance and relationship to their world.

The parents who teach the subtleties of blood-relatedness are thereby helping the child to develop a particularly useful thinking skill, the ability to reason analogically.

We can expect the child to make the necessary transferences:

Oranges are related to lemons; whales are cousins to dolphins; sociology and psychology are sister academic disciplines; theory Y is descended from theory X; archaeology is an offspring of history and of geology; different ideas can be related, can be married.

There is no limit to analogical reasoning. It can take a mind far. A comfortable place to start is in human relationships.[80]

---

80. See Gordon Allport's explanation on page 114.

42

TEACH MANNERS

OF COURSE, CHILDREN learn their manners first and foremost from examples, and only marginally from exhortation.

But the virtue of exhortation is that it speaks to a different part of the brain to reinforce a lesson conveyed in some other, usually non-verbal, manner.

There is a need for a re-awakening of interest in polished manners as exemplified by such newspaper columns such as "Miss Manners" and others. There are "grammars" to human relationships as there are gram-

Figure 44. Universally, manners are a sign of good upbringing. The lack of manners is a sign of neglect. Typically, manners are factored into any opportunity for human relationships, including employment, friendship, and romance.

mars to other forms of communications. It seems rather obvious that the intelligence that all children have will be challenged, not suppressed, if the message is conveyed to them early in their lives: "We expect you to learn the social graces and to manifest them."

What are some of the best ways to teach the so-called "social graces"?

The children's birthday party is, of course, an occasion in which manners are exalted to the forefront of consciousness. We recommend the custom of permitting the children, from about age three, to join the formal "dinner party" or adult party. In Ghana, the children are even taken with the parents to their monthly evening out at the hotel where there is dinner followed by dancing.

Religious ceremonies teach the children the importance of form and order. All tribes have some occasion where that which is valued by the tribe is expressed in non-verbal ceremonial form. The academic graduation ceremony is a popular example of that.

There are hundreds more ways. Whenever the child receives a gift from anyone, a thank-you note is required. Even if the child cannot write, the child can choose the card or the paper and can explain in his or her own words how he or she feels about the gift. The actual writing is secondary to the thought of gratitude.

A child with courteous manners, with some deference to adults, automatically attracts the affection of its elders, each of whom will delight in teaching the child something new. Thus, the courteous or mannerly child has acquired a virtue that attracts other virtues, including knowledge and expert coaching in the complexities of living in an ever-changing world.

43

TREAT THE CHILD AS LEARNER

THE INFANT LEARNS about 60 times faster than an adult, Montessori observed. A child two- or three-years-old learns five or ten times faster than an 18-year-old. If one doubts the accuracy of these statements, we suggest taking one's child on an extended period of residence to, say, Japan or China or Thailand. Even when knowing the language will have "survival" value to the adults in the family, they will take several years to come close to mastering the target language, and with great strain, whereas the child of two to five years will effortlessly master the sound system and other basics of the language in a matter of a few months.

Besides Montessori, another source for these learning rates is the learning curves described in Benjamin Bloom's *Stability and Change in Human Characteristics* (New York: Wiley, 1964). Bloom's work is a "standard" reference and is a required reading in most excellent teacher-training programs. Bloom marshals the empirical and logical evidence to show that learning rates in young children are extraordinary when compared to learning rates in adults. One reason for this is that young children's neural circuitry is open to new learning experiences without pre-conceived notions,

Figure 45. A family we know in Fountain Hills, Arizona, has four children, all straight "A" students, all excellent musicians, all engaged in some community service. One of their secrets? A weekly visit to the library and checking out an average of two books per child. Another is no television in the home.

whereas adults' "computer-like" networks are relatively fixed and much new learning requires "unlearning" some old knowledge or habits.

In addition to possessing the proverbial "clean slate" or *tabula rasa* on which one may write almost anything, the young child is also eager to learn, particularly if his or her environment has a low stress level.

How do we treat the "child as a learner"?

We can discover this by exploring the early childhood of successful people to learn from them some of their secrets. Successful people's parents did just as we are advising: the parents created for the child, who would one day bring distinction upon that family, a miniature library, a miniature museum, a miniature park, a miniature mosque or church, even a miniature classroom or a miniature concert hall. The parents brought the universe to the child.

How does one do this? Take the miniature library: a single parent we know reserves a section of his extensive library for his son. The books are ordered, catalogued. The museum may be only a coin or stamp collection, but it is treated the way a curator treats a prized collection at a major museum – valued and educational, frequently updated and reviewed.

If the family can afford it, we recommend purchasing a musical instrument as soon as possible for the child, as well as a globe and other symbols of the larger universe. The child may also be encouraged to have his or her own little garden, which may be no more than one bean or tomato plant. The child will surprise the parents with what its "absorbent mind" – to use Dr. Montessori's term – can extract from such "living" experiences.

The point is that most cultures still treat a child as if it were passive before the universe. The child's mind is ever active, particularly if the message is conveyed to it: "This is your shelf, take care of the books here." "This is your bean plant, be sure that it gets enough water and air and sunlight," etc.

Obviously, the child is not ready for university-type lectures, nor for the sorts of classroom learning activities common to primary schools. We are not recommending that degree of formality to the learning. But we have learned from the biographical sketches of successful people in many cultures that children ages two and a half to five will astound adults with their abilities to concentrate and to work and to learn if they are engaged in projects of their choosing.

In fact, ambitious parents' efforts in this regard are often misplaced. They want their child to have a "head start" on entering M.I.T. or Tokyo University or some other highly selective institution. So, those ambitious parents teach the child "reading and arithmetic." Sometimes this might be the advisable thing to do, but more likely, those specific skills may wait until the child is five or six years old.

Before formal school-subject matter, there is a whole universe of exciting things to learn. We advise parents to try a variety of activities and allow the child a huge degree of freedom as to the work or play it will engage in. The best guide for the child's learning is the child itself.

Part VIII
Some Specific Suggestions
From Age Three

44

TREAT THE CHILD AS A MATHEMATICIAN
(NOT ARITHMETICIAN)

THE AVERAGE CHILD will not be interested in numbers (1, 2, 3, etc.) nor in manipulating them (adding, subtracting, etc.) at ages three to four. But the child will be keenly interested in other spheres of mathematical thinking and operations:

— *Ratios.* Which block is bigger, longer, heavier, stronger?

— *Conservation of volume.* Will this sand from this cube fit into this cylinder? (The child will not verbalize in this way, but he is training his mathematical sense to make these sorts of hypothetical guesses and he will enjoy testing his hypotheses).

— *Shapes.* The child will love to play with circles, squares, triangles, cubes, pyramids, spheres, cylinders, etc. and study their characteristics – again not arithmetically but geometrically. In effect, the child develops into a "geometer" before he becomes an arithmetician.

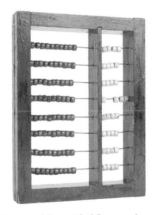

Figure 46. Children who are introduced to a variety of educational devices (such as the abacus) score higher on mathematical aptitude tests than children not so provided. In comparative studies of mathematical achievement, Japanese, Chinese and Korean children score higher than any comparable large groups in the world, in part, because of their "play" or practice with the abacus while young.

— *Tones and Scales.* A xylophone or other simple instrument might be introduced to acquaint the child with musical intervals and other "practical" applications of ratio and proportion. Again, these relationships need not be verbalized. Usually, it is more thrilling and more long-lasting if the child discovers these mathematical relationships for itself.

We urge all parents, if at all possible, to construct for the child a sandbox. It will astound most adults if one were to take the time and list all of the principles of physics a child will learn in the sandbox if he has a few containers and tools and, occasionally, some water. Similarly, a child will often learn some lasting lessons from several commercial toys with mathematical or physics orientations.

If one wishes to pursue this lesson further, we suggest that parents ask their mathematically or scientifically-oriented friends, "How did you develop your talents, your love for mathematics?" Their answers will often serve as a prescription for how any child may be enabled to fall in love with mathematics or any other discipline or profession.[81]

---

81. While many of the best teachers of mathematics are women, many females possess a fear of mathematics. Why so? Partly because many have not had positive experiences with mathematics. The parents can correct this by finding mathematical exercises for the child, many of which are suggested in Piaget. NIM is a classical mathematical game that nearly all children enjoy and that helps the child to associate play and pleasure with mathematical operations.

45

EXPOSE THE CHILD TO SCIENTIFIC PUZZLES

THE CHILD SINCE BIRTH has been presented with one "puzzle" after another: "Where did mother go?" "Who is this other person that draws my mother away from me?" "Where is that light coming from?" "Why does my fist taste so good?"

Cognitively, the infant has not had anything like the "Christmas break" or "spring vacation" or "holiday" that older children seem to require. It would appear that in the early developmental years, the child does not require a mental vacation except sleep and normal rest. The child wants to be busy learning; he intuitively senses that the universe is exceedingly complex, and wishes to get on with the business of mastering that universe. That urge remains strong unless the child is repeatedly discouraged.

Figure 47. Most scientists regard the universe as a giant puzzle, to be investigated and understood. Mentally alert cultures invent puzzles all the time. Healthy families expose the child to as many puzzles as possible, without overwhelming the child. Above, Rubik's cube.

Up until about age two the child's major questions focus on human relationships, language and his immediate environment. From age two and one half to three, the child's interests expand enormously and will know no bounds. At certain stages his interest will focus on plants: trees, shrubs, flowers, fruits, seeds, buds, etc. On occasion, when the child's curiosity is high, each of these should be named and sometimes related: "This bud is a baby flower." "Would you like to take care of that baby tomato plant over there?"

From around age three and one-half the child's abstract ideas and interest in the physical sciences will begin to blossom. Einstein's uncle (or father) gave a compass to young Albert when he was about three or four years old. Prof. Richard Feynman at the California Institute of Technology assuaged the anxieties of his freshman students by telling them that he learned 95% of his physics before he entered school. He was not joking. We suggest to fathers, therefore, that they carefully select or construct several different kinds of learning/puzzling items – preferably one at a time – for their children: mirrors, lenses, magnets in various permutations, swings, sand boxes, wheeled toys such as wagons and tricycles, gyroscopes, kaleidoscopes, telescopes, microscopes, etc.[82]

All of these devices and many others, unless introduced too soon or too overwhelmingly, can help the child become aware that the universe is an open puzzle, not a closed enigma. This realization is the seed that will flower later as a major discovery or a great invention or a powerful idea that will push forward the frontier of human knowledge. The seed of every scientific discovery was, we are persuaded, planted in early childhood.

---

82. Science kits used to be popular gifts for bright children. We urge such gifts by all close relatives.

46

EXPOSE THE CHILD GRADUALLY TO A MULTICULTURAL NURSERY SCHOOL

IN ADDITION TO VERBAL tasks (naming things, learning the rules for complete thoughts) or mathematical tasks (how does the volume remain constant while the shape changes?) or figuring out scientific puzzles (why does the hoop keep rolling even though I stop pushing it?), the child has the enormously complex task of finding ways to get along well with his fellow human beings.

How does one get along with an older brother or an older boy not a close relative? How does a girl get along with a younger child, a girl of the same age but of a different color? How does one relate to a child that is highly talented, say, in music? Or, how does one show friendliness to a teacher of another socio-economic class? These are not easy problems for the child.

Our recommendation: brief (1 to 2 hours) periods of nursery school

Figure 48. When should parents expand the child's understanding that she or he lives in a multi-cultural world society? Most children are ready for this concept by age three to three-and-a-half. Children do not choose to be prejudiced. Children whose early education prepared them for a multi-cultural social environment have no fear of children of different ethnicities and nationalities and therefore establish friendships naturally, not based upon superficial differences. These naturally developed inter-ethnic friendships prepare the child for a global society where almost every organization beyond the family environment is increasingly "international."

from about age 3½ to 4, at least once per week. In many villages of the world, this will occur quite naturally as the mothers gather for community chores or for worship or on festive occasions. In America now more and more religious institutions are establishing "Mothers' Day Off" programs where the mothers leave the children for a little while in a well-equipped setting where there are a large variety of play items while they might accomplish the family shopping or enroll in some self-enrichment course, or conduct some other business. Certainly, most children by that age will have learned to respect the fact that mother has other duties and must leave the child for a short time.

On the positive side, the nursery school, if attended for a short period of time and if well-staffed with trained personnel, can have a beneficial effect. It is healthy for children to see other toddlers and older children performing a variety of activities. Children extract from such observations appropriate notions of what they ought to be able to perform. One of the authors was once consulting with a lady whose eight-month-old child was not yet pulling itself up to stand. The lady was greatly upset because her pediatrician had suggested that the child might be retarded. The fact was that the child was being taken care of by a live-in nanny and thus was not exposed to other children. The infant had no idea that it ought to be standing up by that time.

We recommend that parents choose their nursery school carefully. The reason for this judgment is that child care is enormously expensive. For example, in some states the "standard" is that there be no more than three infants per adult. If each adult were to be earning a mere $15,000 per year, this would mean that each child would have to pay a tuition of $5,000 pro-rated for whatever time the child is in school. It follows that nursery-school personnel often are not well-paid. Therefore many personnel may not have the necessary training and commitment.

Another reason to choose the nursery school carefully is to harmonize the developmental needs of the child with what the nursery school has to offer. A major task of any school today is to teach the human virtues: what used to be called "character training." A nursery school can do this better by example than by exhortation. For example, children at age three will one day be generous and the next day selfish. Child-to-child relationships will be on a roller-coaster, requiring close observations and guidance. If friendships are established at these ages across the racial and national barriers each child so affected will grow to have a much healthier social attitude appropriate to a multi-racial society.

Similarly, it is much easier to appreciate the importance of a culture if a representative of that culture is present and known.

We stress this point because of all the great problems facing the human race, the most urgent, it seems to us, lies in the area of human relations. We think that children without the least trace of racial and cultural prejudice are more likely to solve those human-relations problems than those whose inter-cultural experiences are more limited. The best prevention to racial or cultural prejudice is to have one close friend from a different ethnicity or culture. This will be achieved relatively easily in a well-planned nursery school where several ethnicities and cultures are represented.

47

EXPOSE THE CHILD TO A WIDE VARIETY OF GAMES

THE WORD "GAMES" originally connoted exercises in preparation for aspects of one's life career. Games were nearly always fun and nearly always serious. If one watches children playing games, one can read on their faces a mixture of both fun and seriousness, as well as an intuitive feeling that they know that the games of life are important. Games must never been seen as merely "play" in some negative sense.

Figure 49. Every game trains some aspect of the child's intelligence. Hopscotch trains what Harvard's Howard Gardner calls the Kinesthethic Intelligence, an intelligence that involves physical activity, spatial relationships, and mental challenges. Physics is learned in the sandbox.

The father of the scientific study of children's games and their educational value, the German philosopher Karl Groos, argued that "the preparation for the future can be seen in every game."[83]

Although a few observers of children's play and games have believed that children's games promote the development of their intelligence, that supposition or proposition has been largely unappreciated by educators and

---

83. See also Maxwell, William (Ed.), *Thinking: The Expanding Frontier*. Philadelphia: Franklin Institute Press. 1983.

psychologists until very recently. But despite this apparent blind spot, the universality of children's games has been recognized by a few historians and anthropologists and at least one artist. One of the best expressions of that universality is by Pieter Brueghel's painting, "Children's Games," which is featured in Vienna's Kunst Museum and in many major photographic collections. Brueghel's painting is also frequently used in child development textbooks. Brueghel's painting captured the fact that at the turn from the Middle Ages to the Renaissance European children taught each other their favorite games, thus, we can infer, helping to further cross-fertilize the European intellect. The *Encyclopaedia Britannica* is able to name 30 of the 78 games depicted by Brueghel in 1559. The other games appear to be extinct and no longer played by children.

We list some of those games identified by the *Encyclopaedia Britannica* with the suggestion that parents, nursery school, and school personnel attempt to perpetuate these games, many of which are on the "endangered species" list. A few moments of reflection will reveal the value of each game:

Knucklebones or Jacks	Tug-of-war
Playing with dolls	Odds or evens
Make-believe christening	Running the gauntlet
Carry my lady to London	Blind man's bluff
Hobby horse	King of the mountain
Making mud pies	Stilts
Bowling hoops	Marbles
Playing store	Wrestling
Mumblety-peg	Crack the whip
Building with bricks	Piggyback
Bounce the baby	Whipping tops
Leapfrog	Wedding procession

We share Groos' view that each game teaches one or more psychomotor or social or intellectual skill. For example, bowling hoops teach several principles of physics. A parent can test this proposition by giving a four-and-a-half year old child a metal and bendable hoop to play with. Let the child play with it in a large yard or park for a few minutes. Then, when the child finishes playing with the hoop, the parent should distort the curvature, without letting the child see this happen. The next day, when the child returns to that hoop, the child will, almost automatically, correct the hoop's curvature. In doing so the child will demonstrate silently that he or she learned in a few minutes of play a fundamental law of physics. "The efficiency of a wheel depends upon all radii being of equal length." No one will have lectured the child on this theorem, nor explained the meaning of "radii" or the concept of "equality." The child will have extracted that principle from his play with the hoop.

Similarly, the child will intuitively arrive at other principles of physics from the hoop: inertia, momentum, centripetal force, centrifugal force. And by playing with the hoop, the child will deepen his understanding of the concepts of gravity, friction, the relationship between energy and work, and probably a dozen more concepts.

Each culture invents many games for children, each one of which contains the seeds of ideas and concepts that the child will later find useful in mastering his culture. For example, none of the board games (chess, checkers, Kalah, Nine Men's Morris, etc.) is depicted in *Children's Games*. Yet, each of these not only trains particular intellectual skills, each also trains the powers of concentration and imagination.

Brueghel is communicating another vital historical fact to us: in that period of the 16th Century, there had been, and was to remain for some time, a considerable amount of unity in Europe. The Franks who lived in Britain taught the British children their games and vice versa. The sharing of games and the consequent enlargement of the repertory of games available to all European children may

Figure 50. Children's Games by Pieter Brueghel

have partly contributed to the intellectual eminence of that continent during the last 400 years. Success in any of Brueghel's games required not only mental energy but physical vigor, as well. Feedback as to how one compared with one's fellows must have been almost immediate and abundant.

Now, in the new millennium, the repertory of available children's games has expanded exponentially: we have all the classical board games, plus literally hundreds of recently invented games, including electronic games, nearly every one of which may be in some ways as powerful as bowling hoops in its educational value.[84, 85]

---

84. A good example of the newer type non-electronic game is "Mastermind" which teaches inductive reasoning, the sort of reasoning used by top scientists.

85. See William Maxwell (1983) for a discussion of the world's most popular and IQ-effecting games and his proposed classification system.

48

HAVE A STORY TIME

THE OLD TESTAMENT established the prece-
dent for reading to children and, in effect,
recommends a story time four times a day:

> "And thou shalt teach them diligently
> unto thy children, and shalt talk of
> them (1) when thou sittest in thine
> house, (2) and when thou walkest by
> the way, (3) and when thou liest down,
> (4) and when thou risest up."[86]

As with many children's games, the story
time need not be long, perhaps two to five
minutes. From their earliest ages children
love the discipline of a story time and they
love the warmth that a story conveys, the
sense that one is transmitting all that one
knows and values to a person who will perpetuate that story and history.

*Figure 51. Daily story time has
been found to increase the child's
intelligence and social skills and
increases the strength of the par-
ent-child bond.*

"Story time" dissipates stress and cements
human bonds.

As for which stories to choose, we advise great care in the selection. Analysis of the plots and characters and language of children's stories suggests

---

86. Deuteronomy 6:7. Numeration added for emphasis. Moses was writing particularly
to fathers.

that much information and values are conveyed subliminally to children.[87]

Parents also must be alert to the poor moral messages conveyed in many popular stories.

Our recommendation is relatively easy to execute. A daily story time, perhaps as many as four, if the parents' lifestyle is comfortable with such an arrangement: the story should contain moral or ethical principles that educate the child and be combined with some brief analytical conversation.[88]

---

87. "The Princess and the Pea" a fairy tale by Hans Christian Andersen for example, implies that a royal birth bestows upon one a sensitivity greater than that bestowed upon commoners.

88. See www.gentleplace.com for stories appropriate for children from age six and up.

49

HAVE A MUSIC TIME

SHAKESPEARE WAS RIGHT, music does soothe the savage breast. It refines the soul, disciplines the mind, and studies of the brain show that music also literally lights up the neurons.

Great strides are being made today in understanding how the brain grows and manifests thinking. The studies range from watching how the brain uses oxygen to performing autopsies on the brains of certain animals. The oxygen studies use a mildly radioactive chemical that flows with the oxygen to allow the observer to note which part of the brain is using more oxygen, and which mental task or stimuli engages which part of the brain. These studies are called positron emission tomography (PET scans) and fMRI scans.

Both types of scans literally reveal a section of the brain being lit up like a darkened city coming to life. Those things that light up the brain most effectively include music, intelligent conversation, and some great works of art. Music, particularly baroque

Figure 52. Music represents a balance between all three mental domains of the developing child: psycho-motor (the muscles), affective (the emotions) and the cognitive (the intellectual). Plato, in designing his ideal society, recommended introducing music to children very early. Twenty-four centuries later that advice is still sound. In the future, we assume that all children will be introduced to music by age five. This will have the effect of refining both the intellect and the emotions of future generations.

music, not only lights up the region of the brain responsible for processing sounds, but also lights up other sections that are responsible for abstract and futuristic thought!

Howard Gardner reports that "Fernando Nottebohm has correlated the size of two nuclei in the bird's brain with the appearance of singing. He finds that, during the most productive vocal periods, these two nuclei may become double the size they reach during the least productive period, during the summer molt. Then, when the brain grows larger in the fall, new nerve fibers develop, fresh synapses are formed, and accordingly, a larger song repertoire once again emerges. Apparently, in birds, the learning (or relearning) of a motor activity translates directly into the size of the relevant nuclei, the number of neurons, and the extent of connections among them."[89] Thus, the evidence is strong, not only from birds' brains, but from hundreds of studies of primate and human cortexes, that the brain in both animals and in man expands in structure and in function with positive stimuli.

One of the most powerful stimuli for the brain is music. We therefore recommend that music lessons begin for the child from birth. We would expect the child to begin "performing" musically as soon as it is able to communicate in any other medium. With a simple instrument such as a drum or xylophone, the child will be able to maintain a learned rhythm by age two or two-and-a-half. By the age of three, the child should be ready for a piano, and by three-and-a-half, most children will have matured sufficiently to handle a bow and stringed instrument.

If music is presented to the child naturally, that is, if the child learns to listen to "good" music, the child will naturally wish to *produce* "good" music. Within such a natural musical setting in the home, the issue of "forced" practice and lessons will not arise. The reason that most children have to be "forced" to take music lessons is that the parents missed the key window of opportunity or *sensitive moment* during which the child would have naturally been attracted to the discipline of music. The child willingly embraces music lessons in the first three years of life, and not always in the second three years. [90]

---

89. Howard Gardner, *Frames of Mind: The Theory of Multiple Intelligences.* New York: Basic Books, Inc. 1983, p. 43.

90. See www.suzukiassociation.org for a more thorough discussion of this topic.

50

HAVE A HAPPY HOME

THE INTELLECT, as most other human capacities, flowers in happiness, but in that deep, deep, inner happiness, below the psychological surface where stress and troubles abound. The true inner happiness of man seems to be found only at great depths, down in a region that Carl Jung called the unconscious soul.

All men seek that deep inner peace and happiness where creativity and the intellect seem intimately united. To reach those deep regions of the mind, the individual may often be driven by surface troubles and suffering. Robert Coles, professor of psychiatry at the Harvard Medical School, stated this well at a conference at the Harvard Graduate School of Education in January, 1985: "Why is it that some of the qualities we most admire are to be found in hardship, pain, and suffering?," he asked.

Is it that "hardship, pain, and suffering" drive the soul deep within itself until it finds a region of peace and happiness and in that region discovers the limitless potential of the human intellect?

George Townshend, the late Canon of St. Patrick's Cathedral in Dublin, Ireland, expressed that inevitability of happiness in a different way (1952):

> Happiness is our birth right; it is ours to take, to hold, to possess in perpetuity. If it seems hidden from us it is not hidden by distance but by nearness. It is closer to us than breathing. It is buried in our own hearts; deep, deep in the heart's inmost recesses; and there it dwells waiting . . . to be discovered.

Adler, Alfred, *Understanding Human Nature.* Greenwich, Connecticut, Fawcett, 1927, 1954.

Allport, Gordon, *The Nature of Prejudice.* New York, Perseus Books, 1979.

*Ames, Louise Bates, et. al, *The Gesell Institute's Child from One to Six: Evaluating the Behavior of the Preschool Child.* New York, Harper and Row, 1979.[91]

This publication, representing the most comprehensive observational studies of children ever completed, established what is normal behavior for a child at all ages up to six years, in all domains, psychomotor (ability to crawl, for example); affective (ability to relate to siblings, for example); and cognitive (ability to produce a three-word sentence, for example).

Asimov, Isaac, *Asimov's Chronology of Science and Discovery.* New York, HarperCollins, 1994.

Barnes, P.M., See National Institutes of Health (www.nih.gov), Newsletter Vol. XII, No. 1, Winter 2005.

Bateson, Gregory, *Mind and Nature: A Necessary Unity.* New York. E.F. Dutton, 1977.

Binet, Alfred, *The Experimental Study of Intelligence.* Paris, Ancienne Librairie Schleicher, 1922.

— *A History of Scientific Psychology,* cited in D. B. Klein, New York, Basic Books, 1970, p. 665.

Bloom, Benjamin, *Stability and Change in Human Characteristics.* New York, Wiley, 1964.

---

91. Those starred (*) are recommended for every parent's initial reading/study list.

*Brazelton, T. Berry, *Infants and Mothers: Differences in Development.* New York, Dell Publishing, 1983.

"I would like to see fathers freed as well to be at home and share the responsibility of the early months. But it will be necessary to institutionalize this at the national level. Sweden, Russia, and now Japan have done this already. Otherwise, young parents who take leaves of absence are penalized in the career market. If we believe in families as a nation, we should back them up with just such sanctions." (Epilogue, p. 287)

"Dr. Brazelton has worked with real children over real years of growth in his practice in Cambridge, at the children's Hospital in Boston, and in a variety of long-term studies of growth." (Jerome Bruner in the Foreword) Dr. Brazelton was an Associate Professor of Pediatrics at the Harvard Medical School and a frequent guest on NBC's "Today Show." This book is a must for every parent.

Brookings Institution, Washington, D.C., "A Report on American Family Policy,"1977.

Bruner, Jerome S., *The Process of Education.* Cambridge, Harvard University Press, 1966.

"Experience over the past decade points to the fact that our schools may be wasting precious years by postponing the teaching of many important subjects on the ground that they are too difficult. The reader will find the chapter devoted to this theme introduced by the proposition that the foundations of any subject may be taught to anybody at any age in some form."

Bruner underscores an important point: the child's education is much too important to leave to the public-school teachers. Bruner's classic should be required reading for any educator, including the child's first and most important educators, the parents.

— *On Knowing: Essays for the Left Hand.* Cambridge, MA. Harvard University Press, 1964.

— *Towards a Theory of Instruction.* New York, W. W. Norton, 1968.

*Children's Bureau, Department of Health, Education and Welfare, Publication No. 8, *Infant Care.* Washington, D.C. (20402), Superintendent of Documents, U.S. Government Printing Office. 1967, and subsequently.

*Comer, James P., and Poussaint, Alvin F., *Black Child Care.* New York, Pocket Books, 1976.

Aside from discussing some of the unique problems facing African-American families in the American culture, the book, by two African-American psychiatrists, one at Yale Medical School and the other at the Harvard Medical School, is most valuable to parents of every culture.

"The better you feel about having a baby, the more likely you are to take good care of yourself – which is a good reason to be sure that babies are wanted and pregnancies are planned." (page 19)

Craig, Grace J. and Baucum, Don, *Human Development.* New Jersey, Prince Hall, 2002.

Crain, William, *Theories of Development: Concepts and Applications.* (Fifth Edition). New Jersey, Pearson Prentice Hall, 2005.

DeVos, G. and Wagatsuma, H., *Japan's Invisible Race: Caste in Culture and Personality,* Berkeley, University of California Center for Japanese and Korean Studies, 1966.

Encyclopedia Britannica. (14th Edition) Vol. 4. "Children's Sports and Games."

Encyclopedia Britannica. (14th Edition) Vol. 4. "Public Health Services."

*Erikson, Erik, *Childhood and Society.* New York. W.W. Norton. 1950.

This book is the classic in human development. The eight stages of development outlined in this book predict the psychological evolution of almost every human on the planet:

	Stage	Age	Task or Question;
1	Trust vs Mistrust	birth to one year	"Is the world a safe place?" "Does the Universe love me?"
2	Autonomy vs Shame and Doubt	1 – 3 years	The infant oscillates between being ashamed of his filth and learning how to be autonomous.
3	Initiative vs Guilt	3 – 6 years	The child wrestles with laws and customs that he cannot easily reconcile with his desires.

4	Industry vs Inferiority	6 – 12 years	The child's identity now revolves around his sense of being competent.
5	Ego Identity vs Role Confusion	12 – 18 years	The adolescent crisis of "Who am I?"
6	Intimacy vs Isolation	18 – 40 years	"Success in establishing intimacy is affected by the extent to which the five earlier conflicts have been resolved." Craig, Grace J. and Baucum, Don. *Human Development*. New Jersey, Prentice Hall. 2002, p. 46.
7	Generativity vs Stagnation	40 – 65 years	The individual has an obligation to create something new, or he or she will stagnate.
8	Ego Integrity vs Despair	65 and older	One's life is evaluated critically. Here one prepares for the next life.

Evans, J.L., *Children in Africa: A Review of Psychological Research*. New York, Columbia University, Teachers College Press, 1970.

Evans, Robert, "Reframing the Achievement Gap." *Phi Delta Kappan*. April, 2005.

The essential point of the author is that even the best schooling cannot remediate bad parenting. If we wish to close the achievement gap between African-Americans and other minorities and Whites and Asians we must remediate the source of that gap, unstable families and incompetent parenting.

"Achievement gap critics assume that schooling can exert a powerful transformative impact on large numbers of students. The truth, alas, is that schooling has much less leverage on children than commonly thought. Not just on Hispanic and black students but on all students. In our national debate about school accountability, we have come to equate "education" with "schooling," This is a serious error." (p. 584)

Evans' key point is that children's achievement is far more closely tied to the competency of the parents than to the competency of the school.

Fraser, Diane M. and Margaret Cooper (Eds.), *Myles Textbook for Mid-wives*. Edinburgh, U.K.: Churchill Livingston. 2003.

Furutan, A., *Mothers, Fathers, and Children*. (Translated from the Persian by K. and R. Crerar.) Oxford, U.K., George Ronald, 1980.

"The parents should determine, therefore, to reach mutual agreement on all aspects, whether trivial or important, of child raising. . . . If they are incapable of achieving this objective themselves, they should seek out the assistance of more competent and knowledgeable authorities, and, in full agreement, carry out the resulting decisions . . . so that the children from early childhood consider themselves as being governed by one set plan of action, and see no differences of thought and opinion arising between the parents." (pages 2-3)

Gardner, Howard, *Frames of Mind: The Theory of Multiple Intelligences*. New York, Basic Books. 1983.

Gerber, M., "The Psychomotor Development of African Children in the First Year and the Influence of Maternal Behavior," *Journal of Social Psychology*, 1958. pp. 47, 185-195.

Gilbert, Henry, "Intelligence Tests", *The Encyclopedia of Education,* 1971, Vol. 5

Gilbert, Neil (Ed), *Combating Child Abuse: International Perspectives and Trends*. New York and Oxford: Oxford University Press, 1997.

Glueck, S and Glueck, E., *Delinquents and Nondelinquents in Perspective*. Harvard University Press, 1968.

Groos, K. *The Play of Man*. New York, Appleton, 1901.

This book by the German philosopher is the first known systematic study of children's games, which was later endorsed by Alfred Adler, "The preparation for the future can be seen in every (children's) game."

Hagan, Everett C., *On the Theory of Social Change*. Homewood, IL. The Dorsey Press, 1962.

Haggarty, J.B., "Kalah – The Ancient Game of Mathematical Skill." *In Readings from the Arithmetic Teacher*. S.E. Smith, Jr. and C.A. Beckman (Eds.), Washington, National Council of Teachers of Mathematics. 1979.

Haggarty reported that the game was played at least 5,000 years ago in Sumer (now Iraq), and teaches all of the basic arithmetical concepts pleasurably.

Henry, Jules, "A Cross-Cultural Outline of Education," *Current Anthropology,* Vol. 1, No. 4, July, 1960.

Jensen, Arthur, "How Much Can We Boost IQ and Scholastic Achievement?" *Harvard Educational Review,* Vol. 39, No. 1. Winter 1969, pp. 2-123.

Jensen wrote this article to argue against investing in Head Start, a program where the primary beneficiaries where poor people, especially African-Americans. Jensen's conclusion was that we cannot boost a person's IQ, or only marginally. This position was, of course, refuted by the systematic research of Uri Bronfenbrenner at Cornell and other scholars and by numerous researchers in the immediately subsequent editions of the *Harvard Educational Review.* Jensen's article was noteworthy in an unintended way. The research that he marshaled, read objectively, called into question America's prevailing faith in the power of the schools to remedy bad parenting. Because of the racist implications of Jensen's conclusions, few serious scholars or government policy makers paid much attention to important sets of data presented by Jensen: The fruit of bad parenting will be sour throughout the child's life. Certainly, American policy-makers took no action to remedy the problem that Jensen highlighted.

Herskovitz, Melville, in F.L.K. Hsu (Ed.), *Psychological Anthropology.* Homewood, IL, Dorsey Press, 1961.

Johnson, June, *838 Ways to Amuse a Child.* New York, Collier Books. 1962.

"Crafts, hobbies and creative ideas for the child from six to twelve." (Cover)

Jung, Carl, *Modern Man In Search of a Soul.* London; Routledge & Kegan Paul Ltd. 1933, 1979, pp. 163ff.

*Karmel, Marjorie, *Thank You, Dr. Lamaze.* New York, Harper and Row, 1981.

This, or some similar book on natural childbirth, should be required reading for every intending mother and father.

Kobayashi, Victor N., "Mind and Nature: Teaching and Thinking," in William Maxwell (ed), *Thinking: The Expanding Frontier.* Hillsdale, NJ, Lawrence Erlbaum Publishers, 1983.

*Lamaze, Ferdinand. See www.lamaze.org.

*Leboyer, Frédérick, *Birth Without Violence*. London: Fontana/Collins, 1975.

LeVine, Robert A., "Africa," in F.L.K. Hsu (Ed.), *Psychological Anthropology*. Homewood, IL, Dorsey Press, 1961.

MacKay, D.M., "Cerebral Organization and the Conscious Control of Action," in J.C. Eccles (Ed.), *Brain and Conscious Experience*. New York, Springer. 1966.

Maltz, Maxwell, *Psycho-Cybernetics*. New York, Pocket Books. 1960.

"Confidence is built upon an experience of success." (page 122)

Dr. Maltz, a plastic surgeon, teaches brilliantly the principle of goal-setting and how to build self-esteem. Although not directly concerned with child rearing, the principles given in this book are immediately transferable to that domain.

Marjorie Karmel, *Thank You, Dr Lamaze*. London, Printer & Martin. 2005.

Maslow, Abraham Harold, *Toward a Psychology of Being* (New York, D. Van Nostrand Co., Second Edition, 1968).

Maxwell, William (Ed.), *Thinking: The Expanding Frontier*. Philadelphia, Franklin Institute Press. 1983. (Now published by Lawrence Erlbaum, at Hillsdale, NJ).

Although addressed to researchers and policy-makers primarily, the book has at least four chapters that will be useful to parents, particularly the chapter on children's games, which propounds a theory of learning that is immensely optimistic.

— *A Challenge to the Black Superintendent*, *Phi Delta Kappan*, Vol. LVI, No. 8, April, 1975.

— *Is the IQ Any Good Any More?* A paper delivered at the Convention of the American Association of School Administrators, Minneapolis, Minnesota, U.S.A., July 9, 1978.

— "Games Children Play, Powerful Tools that Teach some Thinking Skills", in Maxwell, William (Ed.), *Thinking: The Expanding Frontier*. Hillsdale, NJ, Lawrence Erlbaum Publishers. 1983.

— *Experiments on Improving Mental Abilities in Children*. Suva, Fiji, School of Education, The University of the South Pacific, 1981.

McClelland, David C., *The Achieving Society*. New York, The Free Press. 1961.

Social psychologist McClelland re-states the basic thesis of Max Weber that the world view of a culture operating through the family in the family's child rearing practices ultimately determine if the culture is a high or a low achieving culture. Alas, most human cultures today are notoriously low achieving because they have not recognized this chain of causation or done very little about it. The exceptions appear on every list of "healthy societies," the Scandinavian countries, Singapore, etc. Another technical book written for other scholars. But it is a principal source to understand motivation and achievement. Readable by the average motivated parent.

McDonough, Siobhan (Associated Press), "Incarceration rate rising since 2000," published in the *Arizona Republic*, April 25, 2003 (page A7).

"The United States has a higher rate of incarceration than any other country. . . . There were 725 inmates for every 100,000 U.S. residents by June 30, 2004. An estimated 12.6 percent of all black men in the late 20s were in jails or prisons, as were 3.6 percent of Hispanic men and 1.7 percent of white men in that age group. . . ."

*Montessori, Marie, *The Secret of Childhood*. (M. J. Costelloe, S.J., Tr.) New York, Ballantine, 1972.

This book is a classic in early-childhood education. If it is not available in one's local library, one should insist that it become available. In the meantime, one should read other books by or about Dr. Maria Montessori, Italy's first female physician. No one's education today is complete unless one is familiar with the insights of this education pioneer.

— *The Absorbent Mind*. New York, Dell Publishing, 1984.

This book is a *tour de force* of astute observations that led Dr. Montessori to her views that the child is a spiritual being from the beginning of its life.

*Morris, Desmond, *Babywatching*. New York, Crown Publishers. 1992.

This author of *The Naked Ape* is one of the most astute observers of human behavior. Morris' eyes are almost as keen as Darwin's.

Newberg, Andrew; D'Aguili, Eugene D.; Rause, Vince, *Why God Won't Go Away*. New York; Ballantine Publishing. 2001.

*Pearce, Joseph Chilton, *Magical Child*. New York, E. P. Dutton, 1977.

This is another brilliant work that marshals the evidence to assert that all children are born geniuses. Easy to read and very future oriented.

Pettigrew, Thomas, *A Profile of the Negro American,* Princeton, Van Nostrand, 1964.

Phillips, John L. Jr., *The Origins of Intellect: Piaget's Theory.* San Francisco, W. H. Freeman. 1975.

This book was written for university educational psychology students and students in cognitive psychology and is understandable by motivated parents. Piaget's theories now provide the principal guides to pioneering practitioners and researchers in early-childhood development.

"It is absolutely impossible to dispense logico-mathematical knowledge." (page 145)

"Whether the learner is a child, an adolescent, or an adult; whether the knowledge is social, physical or logico-mathematical; a person who acquires knowledge must be active." (page 141)

Piaget, Jean. *Play, Dreams and Imitations in Childhood.* (C. Gattegno and F. M. Hodgson, Trs.) New York, Norton Library, 1962.

Pinneau, Samuel R. *Changes in Intelligence Quotient.* Boston, Houghton Mifflin, 1961.

This is a report of the largest and longest running longitudinal study of IQs. Every white person born in Berkeley, California, in the year 1929, was invited to return to the campus of the university there every year to re-take the "gold standard" of IQ tests, the Stanford-Binet. The idea was to see how stable IQs are or how much IQs fluctuate. The answer: The average fluctuation was 10 – 14 points. The least fluctuation was six points. The most was forty. Thus, there has never been a research study (except the faked studies of Sir Cyril Burt at London University) that showed IQs to be unchanging. Not only are IQ scores ever-changing, we can predict with relative certainty the direction of those changes. Family stability and intellectual stimulation, among many other factors, promote improvements in IQ scores; divorce and stress and many other variables decrease IQ scores.

Ridley, Matt, *Genome: The Autobiography of a Species in 23 Chapters.* New York, Harper/Collins Publishers. 1999.

"Man with all his noble qualities still bears in his bodily frame the indelible stamp of his lowly origin." Charles Darwin, cited on page.23. "While fossil records are a wonderful place to study human evolution, the essence of this book is that our genes tell the story of our species' development more infallibly."

— *Nature Via Nurture.* New York, Harper/Collins Publishers. 2003.

"Do parents have any important long-term effects on the development of their child's personality? This article examines the evidence and concludes that the answer is no." Judith Rich Harris writing in the prestigious *Psychological Review*, cited by Ridley, p. 251.

*Roe, Anne, *The Making of a Scientist*. New York, Dodd Mead. 1963.

*Rosenthal, Robert, and Jacobson, Leonore, *Pygmalion in the Classroom*, New York, Holt, Rinehart and Winston, 1968.

Rosenthal's and Jacobson's research probably has done more than any other study to dissipate that false image that one's IQ is fixed. "The Pygmalion Effect" or the "Rosenthal Effect" says that if a significant person (parent, teacher, etc.) tells a child that she is "bright" or "dull" that prediction becomes a self-fulfilling prophecy. Even if the significant person does not "tell" the child his belief or prediction, but actually thinks that the child will be dull because of caste or appearance or other irrelevant variable, that prediction too tends to become self-fulfilling.

Scarne, John. *Encyclopedia of Games*. New York, Harper and Row, 1973.

Tiger, Lionel and Shepher, Joseph. *Women in the Kibbutz,* New York, Penguin, 1977.

Townshend, George, "The Wellspring of Happiness," in *The Mission of Bahá'u'lláh and other Literary Pieces.* Oxford, England, George Ronald Publishers. 1952.

Walter, Duncan, See www.nih.gov, "Prayer and Spirituality in Health: Ancient Practices, Modern Science" Newsletter. Vol XII. No. 1, Winter, 2005.

"Waterbirth" at www.waterbirthinfo.com.

Whimbey, Arthur, *Intelligence Can Be Taught*. New York, E. P. Dutton. 1980.

"A quarter of a century ago, (Benjamin) Bloom and (Lois) Broder reported a study that should have served as a model for a new wave of research in training mental ability. The time, however, was not ripe. Bloom and Broder's approach ran contrary to the existing traditions in American psychology. Moreover, when the study was conducted (1945 to 1950) the question of whether academic aptitude could be improved through special training had not yet become a focus of national concern" (page 53).

Whimbey is another pioneer in inventing ways to help students, especially university students, learn how to think logically and creatively, particularly in mathematics.

*White, Burton L., *The First Three Years of Life*. New York, Avon Books, 1984.

"Since 1958, supported by several large private foundations and federal agencies, and assisted by several dozen talented people, I have studied the problem of how to educate babies. To my knowledge, no other individual researcher has studied the problem of influencing the development of abilities in the first three years of human life so extensively. . . .What follows does come from a unique source: the most sustained (and expensive) scientific study of the role of experience in the development of human abilities in the first years of life conducted to date." (From the book, The Preface, p. xiii).

— *Educating the Infant and Toddler*. Lexington, MA. D.C. Heath and Company, 1988.

World Health Organization, *Evidence for the Ten Steps to Successful Breast-feeding* (WHO/CHD/98.9), 1998. 117 pages (U.S. $10.) (WHO Order No. 1930142)

— *Infant Feeding: The Physiological Basis*. 1990. 108 pages. ISBN 92 4 068670 3. U.S.$18.00 (WHO order No. 0030701)

— *Promoting Breast-feeding in Health Facilities: A short Course for Administrators and Policy Makers*. 1996. 391 pages. US$162 (WHO Order No. 1930100)

— *Protecting, Promoting and Supporting Breast-feeding: The Special Role of Maternity Services: A Joint WHO/UNICEF Statement*. 1989, iv + 32 plates. ISBN 92 4 156130 0 US$5.40. (Who Order No. 1150326)

Figure 1. Short-Wavelength Infrared View of Galaxy Messier 81, NASA Jet Propulsion Laboratory (NASA-JPL).

Figure 7. Geneticist Dr. Theodosius Dobzhansky, Courtesy: Rockefeller University Archives.

Figure 17. Pregnant Mother on Birthing Stool, Image from a 15th-century woodprint in a book by Eucharius Roeslin.

Figure 20. Neuron (Illustration)

Figure 27. Infant Breast-feeding, Kathleen Finlay (Masterfile)

Figure 34. Family Reunion, Kevin Dodge (Masterfile)

Figure 47. Rubic's Cube, (stock xchng, www.sxc.hu)

Figure 50. Children's Games by Pieter Brueghel, Courtesy Kunsthistorisches Museum, Vienna, Austria.

Figures 31, 32 (Comstock)

Figures 2-6, 8-13, 15, 19, 26, 29, 40, 45, 46, 49, 51 (Photos.com)

Figures 14, 16, 18, 21-25, 28, 30, 33, 35-39, 41-44, 48, 52 (Alamy)

Professor William Maxwell, Ed.D., is one of two professors of thinking in the world. He has taught at universities on five continents, beginning in 1954 in Korea. In 1970 he was the first principal of the first post-secondary school in southeastern Nigeria, the Advanced Teacher Training College, Port Harcourt. He also has served as dean of schools of education at California State University, Fresno and the University of the South Pacific, Suva, Fiji. He was awarded his current title by the University of Advancing Technology in May of 2004.

Dr. Maxwell's research studies on intelligence and curriculum development have been published in Korea (*Sasaengye* (Intellectual World)), France (UNESCO's *Prospects in Education*), Australia, Nigeria, Fiji, Britain, and in several journals in the United States, including in *Phi Delta Kappan* and a chapter in *Developing Minds* published by the Association for Supervision and Curriculum Development. His book, *Thinking: The Expanding Fronti*er, (Lawrence Erlbaum, 1983) was selected for the recommended reading list on thinking at the Harvard Graduate School of Education Library.

Professor Maxwell's most significant work was the supervised research of his experienced teachers, drawn from all over the South Pacific, at the University of the Pacific. Those research studies demonstrated that children's intelligence scores are substantially enhanced by daily regimes of mental exercises.

While at the University of the South Pacific, he founded the International Conference on Thinking, which was the world's first academic conference focused on teaching the thinking processes, where all disciplines from anthropology to mathematics to zoology participated.

William graduated valedictorian from Phoenix's Carver High School and attended Howard, Oregon State, California (Berkeley), Maryland, Oxford and Harvard universities. His masters and doctorate in education were earned at Harvard University. He was recently awarded the honorary title of Professor of Education and Educational Psychology Emeritus by Ottawa University.

Mary Elizabeth Maxwell received her training in public health nursing at St. Elizabeth's Hospital in Washington, D.C, and at the Francis Payne

Bolton School of Nursing at Case Western Reserve University, Cleveland. Her first public health assignments were in a district of Cleveland where most of her patients were recent immigrants from Eastern Europe. Mary was later hired by the Bureau of Indian Affairs to serve the Bannock and Shoshone tribes of Idaho where she advised mothers of newborns, supervised quarantines, and assisted patients to obtain appropriate health care.

From Idaho she accepted a position as Chief Nursing Education Supervisor for the U.S. Trust Territory School of Nursing, Koror, Palau, Caroline Islands, where she taught nursing and public health to the four-year students which she recruited from all of the islands of the U.S. Trust Territories of the Pacific. With her husband, William, Mary also lived and studied in Korea, Nigeria and Fiji and traveled to all parts of the world with him, frequently lecturing on health and education issues. Mary Maxwell passed away on September 9, 2001.

Ruth Leilani Smith, a native of Chicago, Illinois, earned her Bachelor of Arts. in English Literature at Illinois Wesleyan University, and a Master of Arts in Tourism and Special Event Management from Canterbury University, United Kingdom. Leilani is an administrative and travel professional, realtor, and teacher of adults with disabilities.

Leilani is a founding director of the Council for a Parliament of the World's Religions, and is listed in the 1999 *Who's Who in Business*. She is a co-founder of the Vanguard of the Dawning Project, a national organization devoted to empowering minorities through educational activities and international service projects.

Leilani taught English as a Second Language in Portugal for four years, and served as a volunteer in Haifa, Israel for two years. She has travelled and lectured widely in the Americas, Africa, Europe and the South Pacific. She currently resides in south Florida.

Jim Pearce was born in the Republic of South Africa. He moved to the United States in 1984 where he married Sabrina Sullivan, the mother of their three daughters, Lindsay, Kayla and Rachel. He received a Master's Degree in Marriage and Family Therapy in 1991, from Abilene Christian University. In the mid nineties, he began his career in technology, working as a Web developer with a major medical practice management software company in Ridgefield, Connecticut. In 2002, he joined the faculty of the University of Advancing Technology in Tempe, Arizona where he teaches web design and development as well as 2D graphic design.